Delivering Effective Behaviour Support in Schools

A Practical Guide

GILES BARROW

David Fulton Publishers
London

David Fulton Publishers Ltd
Ormond House, 26–27 Boswell Street, London WC1N 3JZ

www.fultonpublishers.co.uk

First published in Great Britain by David Fulton Publishers 2002

Note: The right of Giles Barrow to be identified as the author of this work has been asserted by him in accordance with the Copyright, Designs and Patents Act 1988.

Copyright © Giles Barrow 2002

British Library Cataloguing in Publication Data
A catalogue record for this book is available from the British Library.

ISBN 1–85346–796–0

Typeset by FiSH Books, London
Printed in Great Britain by Bell & Bain Ltd, Glasgow

Contents

To the team, wherever you may be out there tinkering within the system, many thanks for your inspiration, collaboration and most of all the humour.

Acknowledgements

I would like to thank Eddie McNamara and Mark Jolly for granting me permission to use their invaluable *Towards Better Behaviour* material. In addition, Chris Watkins not only gave me permission to use his excellent material, but made an early impact on my thinking when I first entered into the world of behaviour support for which I am especially grateful. Thanks must also go to Trudi Newton for providing specific support and advice regarding theoretical input relating to material in the second chapter on engaging effectively with schools. Pete Hrekow and Paul Howard have also been generous in allowing me to use material from other publications in addition to their being a terrific pair of colleagues. My thanks also go to the David Fulton team for their support during the planning and drafting of my writing and especially my editor, Jude Bowen.

I am tremendously grateful for the contributions made by a number of services and specifically Keith Elliott and Katherine Bridges from Gloucester, Kate Evans from Sutton LEA and Emma Bradshaw from the Sutton Primary Behaviour Support Team. I also thank Peggy Gosling for allowing me to use material from her own study into effective behaviour support.

Finally, I need to record my thanks for my own children's patience and to Jackie, my wife, who spent longer than I proof-reading the text.

Introduction

Why write a book on behaviour support?

When I started out in behaviour support I was thrilled to be given a chance to save youngsters from being excluded. Off I would go, racing from school to school on my motorbike, turning up like emergency service personnel and dishing out conflict resolution to kids as if it were going out of fashion. In hot pursuit of an exclusion waiting to happen, I patrolled the corridors and stock cupboards of local schools working with kids who had been targeted for support from Mr Behaviour Man.

Far from being deranged and dangerous, the majority of the children I worked with were tired, despairing, underachieving and invariably desperately sad about their circumstances. They had a bundle of other stuff on their minds which had little to do with individual teachers but more to do with a general disaffection from conventional teaching and learning, with a good measure of domestic hassle thrown in.

Only in retrospect do I now recognise that the same might have been said of many of the staff who referred the pupils. They too expressed exhaustion, feelings of inadequacy and a sense of alienation from the demands of an increasingly utilitarian educational system. So often it was not the kids, but the changing demands made on their role, the poor communication or mismanagement of the organisation that lay at the centre of their frustration. However, my task in those early days was to fix the kids and so off I went bouncing into the broom cupboard to teach another Year 11 pupil school survival skills.

I suppose it took a couple of years before I began to make a different sense of listening to children and teachers talking about problem behaviour. The penny dropped one day when a youngster told me that in his view half the teachers at the school needed referring to a behaviour support service. He reckoned they could do with a dose of the kind of work he had been involved with. Why was it that all my efforts were focused on the pupil? How was it that I spent my time listening to stories told by both pupils and teachers about getting stuck on behaviour, but it was always the kids that got time-out to think about solutions? Could this be related to why it was so difficult to sustain success after closing cases – because teachers had not had the opportunity to reflect on responding differently?

I have the good fortune to work regularly with colleagues involved in delivering behaviour support and I am struck by how familiar the experience of working with one half of a solution is for support teams. Over the past decade we have been struggling to address an interminable dilemma. If we assume that all behaviour is linked to context, how is it that behaviour support so often seeks to remedy child-based difficulties, and so rarely involves substantial efforts to change the systems in which teachers and pupils work together?

Often in my work with behaviour support services I ask colleagues the extent to which they have arrangements for referring and managing individual pupil work. In all cases I am told of complex, highly detailed procedures to ensure that support is directed at the right children. When I ask how non-pupil-based work is generated, if at all, I tend to be met with a thoughtful silence. The tendency around the country is for behaviour support to focus primarily on pupil-based intervention. Where systems work is developed it is generally triggered through an ad hoc, informal connection, sometimes as an afterthought. In very few services does professional development form the predominant intervention, even if its impact is acknowledged as an aim of the service.

One of the reasons for writing this book is to share the experience of behaviour support teams which have found interesting paths into working with systems and have formed a different balance in their work, where intervention increasingly focuses on changing problem behaviour, not simply the behaviour of children.

My second reason for writing the book is to understand the changing context in which behaviour support is now developed and delivered. When I first began planning this book the world of behaviour support was a little simpler. In the late 1990s the majority of support was delivered by central local education authority (LEA) services with a smaller level of support provided on an outreach basis by special schools and Pupil Referral Units (PRUs). Over the past three years there have been dramatic changes in policy and funding arrangements which have created a far more fragmented picture.

The early political agenda of the Conservative administration to establish schools – especially secondary schools – as autonomous has been hotly pursued by the more recent Labour administrations, and this has been in part reflected by the increased delegation of funds direct to school budgets. Furthermore, the emerging role of LEAs in the 'new order' indicates little opportunity or endorsement for maintaining peripatetic support services, once again especially with regard to the secondary sector. The pressure on LEAs is to monitor performance, broker funding and coordinate activity, and is less on delivering services. Even in the area of pupil welfare and provision for pupils educated otherwise than at school, the developing picture shows LEAs maintaining responsibility for ensuring that these areas are addressed, but not necessarily through providing the service itself.

Over the past year alone a number of peripatetic services have closed due to the shift in policy and funding. Several of these teams have a longstanding record of success and unfortunately this has counted for precious little in the eyes of authorities anxious to follow the lead towards delegation of budgets. Where services continue, often at reduced staffing levels, the tendency is increasingly on deploying staff into local schools where there are concerns about performance.

For those colleagues working in outreach services a similar squeeze has also been reported by staff in PRUs. Whereas this work has often been the result of a canny juggle between support to schools and providing education programmes for pupils on site, this has become increasingly difficult to maintain in moving towards full-time provision for excluded pupils. Again, the remit of behaviour support has been significantly limited in terms of time and resourcing.

Readers might assume from these comments that behaviour support has a poor future, that its demise is imminent (and that the rationale for this book is somewhat redundant!). However, there have been parallel developments in terms of national policy that have had quite the reverse impact on behaviour support. The social inclusion agenda has gathered apace since 1999 when the work of the Social Exclusion Unit began to indicate the government's intentions for the area of education. The then DfEE guidance for schools and LEAs on social inclusion presented a number of significant challenges, most notably for the LEA in terms of providing full-time education for excluded pupils and for schools to reduce the level of truancy and exclusion. (Readers will be aware that while the requirement regarding full-time provision remains unchanged for LEAs, there has been a series of modifications to exclusion procedures to accommodate the anxieties of head teachers, indicating the political sensitivities around behaviour support work.)

With the new guidance and legislation has come a substantial level of funding in the form of the Standards Fund and the Excellence in Cities (EiC) programmes. Once again readers may be familiar with many of the national initiatives and their local derivations. Learning Support Mentors, Learning Support Units, supported reintegration programmes, home-school workers, school-based youth workers, alternative curriculum programmes and improved electronic systems for monitoring pupil attendance and behaviour are a handful of examples of the types of activities that schools have been encouraged to develop. Just outside of the immediate parameters of school-based initiatives there have also been the national reviews of careers and youth services. The more recent introduction of the Connexions Service for young people and the setting up of the Children and Young People's Unit, with its own substantial funding programme, indicate that there are resources for dealing with disaffection for some time to come. Likewise, the introduction of early years planning and resourcing of particular programmes such as Sure Start and On Track indicate a similar security for work with younger children and their families.

However, my own belief is that the funding is intended and directed far less to local authorities, but to service providers, some of which are the schools themselves, but many of which use local schools as the arena for delivering support. The growth in the involvement of the private and voluntary sector in supporting schools in the field of behaviour has been considerable. A number of small partnerships, companies, charities and community groups are now busily involved in working with pupils in schools. Often this work might be funded by the LEA but in these situations it is clear that service provision is no longer the job of the authority.

The need for behaviour support services is not in decline. Anecdotal evidence, reports from head teacher and professional conferences demonstrate that the need for support on school behaviour issues is as high as it has ever been. What have changed over the past couple of years are the channels through which support is coordinated and delivered. For example, many colleagues who were once working in LEA behaviour support teams in the past have now been appointed by schools as coordinators for learning mentors, teachers-in-charge of units, or employed in the voluntary sector to deliver projects with groups of pupils. Behaviour support is not dead, it is just increasingly wearing a different outfit.

I believe that there are implications for behaviour support practice as a result of these changes, especially in terms of professional support and service quality, hence the reason for writing this book. As behaviour support is delivered across a range of providers, the capacity to build up and extend local expertise in behaviour support planning and practice becomes limited. Individual support teachers working in schools repeatedly tell stories of isolation and inadequate supervision. Similarly their capacity to *challenge* and support schools to improve is significantly limited. In doing so, schools deny themselves the potential for effective intervention while individual staff feel estranged.

Another implication of the fragmentation of services is that the behaviour support community becomes even more difficult to address in terms of professional development. For years behaviour support staff have had very little training aimed at their distinctive needs. The tendency has been for teams to attend courses intended for special educational needs coordinators (SENCOs) or other mainstream colleagues. While this can often be useful it rarely addresses the particularly difficult issues of working in a supporter role in the field of behaviour. One of the few opportunities is the excellent national behaviour support conference hosted by Peter Gray through New Directions in Behaviour Support. There are some regional networking events and in London the work of Peter Hrekow for the Special Educational Needs Joint Initiative for Training (SENJIT) has been important in providing training for support teams. Only one of the professional associations – the National Union of Teachers – has begun to develop training specifically for members from behaviour support services. Given the number of teachers involved nationally in peripatetic work, it is a little surprising that professional associations offer very little dedicated training for this group of members.

Not only is there little dedicated training for behaviour specialists but also there is not a great deal of published material. Once again there are plenty of resources for teachers on behaviour but these do not pick up the issues for those delivering support. There are some notable exceptions; Mark Provis' book on systemic intervention, *Dealing with Difficulty* (Provis 1992), is an excellent book, although unfortunately now out of print! Work by Gray, Miller and Noakes (Gray *et al.* 1994) also includes useful discussion about service delivery but most other material is tucked into association journals, for example *Pastoral Care in Education*. So, another important reason for writing a book on behaviour support was to respond to the need for professional development material for those colleagues in behaviour support.

Who is this book for?

It was initially assumed that the prime audience for the book would be colleagues working in LEA behaviour support services and those delivering outreach support from special schools and PRUs. However, given the comments above, this focus has now been significantly widened. It is anticipated that all teachers and non-teachers delivering behaviour support will find the material interesting. Mentors, learning support unit teams, colleagues working in voluntary sector or private partnerships will hopefully pick up ideas for training school staff or supporting the development of project work in schools.

Colleagues working in learning support services, educational psychology services and school advisory and inspection services may also find the ideas about service development and operational aspects of interest. While the principles of working at a systems level in schools have been obviously pegged onto the field of behaviour, underlying systemic principles remain the same.

The book is especially written for those services that are not only delivering behaviour support but are interested in developing a particular model, namely one that addresses systemic change. For this group of readers the book offers case study material from around the country where behaviour support has been predominantly focused on changing the systems that impact on the behaviour of adults and children in schools.

It is worthwhile at this stage pointing out that this book has not been written for teachers looking at developing their behaviour management skills. Neither is the book about dealing with disruptive pupils or how to develop whole-school policy and practice. It offers little about classroom leadership in relation to behaviour and there is only brief consideration given to general perspectives on behaviour. This book is not about behaviour management! There is plenty of good material already on the market on this subject. Instead the aims of the book relate more to professional development for support teams and service management issues for delivering behaviour support.

How to use the book

It is unlikely that the reader will sit and read this book in sequential order but will probably prefer to dip into sections. While the book is intended to be treated as an incremental approach to setting up and delivering effective support work, it is possible to be selective in reading sections. The book is split into five chapters and the following provides an overview of contents and tips for possible use.

Chapter 1: Effective behaviour support presents a best practice model for delivering systemic behaviour support. The section covers some general observations about the history of behaviour support and reflections on conventional practice in behaviour support services, before looking in detail at the principles and initial planning for setting up systemic behaviour support work. The section includes consideration of staff roles, responsibilities and professional development issues. Perhaps most importantly this section includes discussion about the way in which effective behaviour support is linked to the school improvement agenda.

This section is a good starting point for those in the early stages of setting up services, or who have the opportunity to review existing support arrangements. The section on school improvement links will be of interest to those interested in working in partnership with advisory and inspectorate services.

Chapter 2: Getting started is subdivided to include a section on contracting and another on referral and assessment. The material on contracting includes key principles for setting up effective partnership work with schools and examples of pro formas and case study material illustrating theory into practice. The section covering referral and assessment considers specific techniques and procedures for identifying and generating systemic behaviour support work. Once again, references to valuable material are given, pro formas and case study material included.

For readers frustrated with existing arrangements where they feel overwhelmed by numbers of pupils being referred or struggling with waiting lists, this chapter offers some useful observations and resources.

Chapter 3: Delivering effective behaviour support looks in more detail at the practical issues of providing systemic intervention with schools. Ideas for working with different staff groups, supporting whole-school development and specific approaches to working at the sharp end of individual casework, including exclusion and reintegration, are covered.

For established services and readers familiar with behaviour support work this section may offer some new spins on familiar ideas. For those new to support work there is a range of practical ideas to use in working systemically with staff and pupils.

Chapter 4: Monitoring and evaluation considers how team managers can set up procedures for measuring and reviewing service performance from a systemic perspective. Although written with team managers in mind, the section will be useful to all team members in terms of raising awareness about the particular aspects of this area of support work.

The final chapter of the book, **Chapter 5: Behaviour support: possibilities**, considers the future for behaviour support and offers suggestions for how effective support might be sustained over the coming years.

1 Effective behaviour support

This section describes a model for establishing an effective behaviour support service. The model presented is based on systems theory and an explanation of the key principles of the approach are covered before a detailed account of how these can influence the shape of behaviour support work. The section includes case study material to illustrate the process of turning theory into practice and draws on the experience of services around the country that use a systems approach to service delivery. This approach is explained later but essentially results in prioritising intervention at whole-school and professional development as opposed to a major emphasis on addressing difficulties with individual pupils.

In addition to theoretical and operational aspects of support, the section also considers the links between behaviour support and the school improvement agenda. Finally, this section also provides some resource material and ideas for professional development for behaviour support teams.

Introducing systems theory

Let me begin by presenting my understanding of systems theory and what it means for behaviour support. For many years the principles of systems theory have guided significant developments in non-educational fields, most notably family therapy. The theory and its early application emerged during the late 1960s and was based on the work of Bertalanffy (Bertalanffy 1968). The development of systems theory in the field of education has perhaps been most associated with the work of Alex Molnar and Barbara Lindquist (Molnar and Lindquist 1989). Their work was drawn from experience in the United States that focused on changing problem behaviour in schools and which the authors named the **ecosystemic perspective**. For the purposes of my work it has been this material that has proven to be the most influential in my thinking about developing behaviour support.

The underlying principle of ecosystemic theory is straightforward enough; problem behaviour 'is part of, not separate from the social setting within which it occurs' (Molnar and Lindquist 1989). A critical emphasis is that problem behaviour has two elements: the behaviour itself and the range of perceptions about the behaviour. For instance, quiet talking in class is a behaviour that is not a problem in many classes. However, if a teacher has demanded silence, then pupils' quiet talking will be perceived as problem behaviour. Ecosystemic practitioners are as curious about perceptions as they are about actual behaviour.

Ecosystemics offers very rich territory for the behaviour support specialist, not least because of its distinctive characteristics:

- It focuses directly on change in the problem situation rather than on the diagnosis of the problem individuals.
- It does not require elaborate or exhaustive plans either to replace or to supplement current practice. The ideas can be readily and comfortably employed by educators who have different styles and work in a variety of settings.
- It enables educators to start small with manageable aspects of problems.
- It encourages divergent explanations for problem behaviour.
- It encourages light-heartedness and open-mindedness in the face of chronic problems.
- It is designed to build on strengths, not to overcome deficits.
- The ideas can be mastered without any specialised background knowledge. (Molnar and Lindquist 1989)

I find these features both refreshing but also reflect an optimism about the capacity for change and growth, both of which are arguably sound values on which to build behaviour support. From an ecosystemic perspective the school provides a significant system within a series of other systems which can include families and peer groups, other services and schools. When we consider behaviour there is a range of different levels at which behaviour happens:

- behaviour between children;
- behaviour between children and families;
- behaviour between children and teachers;
- behaviour between teachers and teachers;
- behaviour between teachers and non-teachers;
- behaviour between staff and schools;
- behaviour between schools and services;
- behaviour between services and local authorities, etc., etc.

While these levels are presented as a list, the reality of our experience is that there is an interrelatedness between these levels. So, from an ecosystemic perspective, the behaviour of a child in the classroom is best understood in the context of the child's perceptions about the class – his or her peers, teachers, school – and the perceptions of the child by parents, teachers and peers. This intricate web of relationships is the *ecosystem* in which behaviour takes place and is the arena through which behaviour takes its meaning.

What has fascinated me most about applying this theory is in looking at the *organisational* behaviour of support services and most significantly behaviour support services. Whether we are aware of it or not, our support service *behaves*, and this is determined in part by our perceptions about our world and the perceptions about us of others. This principle applies whether we are working from a pupil referral unit, special school, LEA team or in-school centre. How we decide to operate gives out messages to others about our beliefs and values.

What I have most valued about applying systems theory to behaviour work is that it has provided opportunities to systematically support the development of genuine, sustainable change in problem behaviour. It is an approach that preserves the dignity of children and adults and encourages growth and understanding. Once again, these are arguably sound values on which to establish a behaviour support service.

Three in one: introducing a three-dimensional approach to behaviour support

> Understanding problem behaviour will not be found by focusing on the child, nor by focusing on the school, but the study and analysis of *the interactions between them.* (Faupel 1990)

This is a great line; it defines precisely the prime territory for effective behaviour support: 'the interactions' between school, teacher, class/group and individual pupil. Note the subtle use of language – Faupel is clear in deterring specialists from falling into an either/or trap; either it is the child's fault or the teacher's. Many staff working in specialist support services are well aware of the limitations of child-deficit approaches in which intervention is focused on 'healing' inherent deficiencies. Unfortunately a consequence can be that teachers and schools are cited as the cause of difficulty. This is an equally limited view and simply involves managing a different sphere of dysfunction. Working effectively in behaviour support is about heading out into an alternative direction which seeks to unblock limitations of systems, perceptions and intentions.

The three dimensions of effective behaviour support

If behaviour support is to reflect the principles of systems theory then a careful balance must be struck in how support is generated, targeted and delivered. The tendency has been for support services to orientate their work predominantly on children. This is understandable for at least two reasons.

- First, there is a longstanding tradition in UK education for schools to identify pupils with needs as a means of securing additional support. Special educational needs (SEN) and pastoral support protocols both nationally and at regional level promote the child-deficit mindset that is so entrenched in the British system.
- Second, school-focused intervention has tended to be the territory of subject advisors and inspectorate teams. Invariably these teams have provided a subsidiary role in relation to behaviour support on the premise that behaviour has actually meant *pupil* behaviour, which has been tucked into SEN or pupil welfare services, not school improvement divisions.

The upshot of this history is that behaviour support generally has been triggered through the identification of disruptive children and resulted in pupil-centred intervention. The challenge for the systems theorist is to crack the convention and develop a radical alternative brand of support.

In taking on this challenge the effective behaviour support service might start with the aim to maximise schools' capacity to promote and respond to behaviour. The objectives of effective behaviour support might be best defined as follows (in order of priority):

1. To support the development of whole-school policy and approach.
2. To provide professional development for adults working within the school.
3. To offer holistic intervention in relation to individual pupils.

Several behaviour support services already have similar objectives which are explicitly shared by members of the support team and/or schools. Effective behaviour support means delivering intervention in a way that directly reflects the intended aims of the service. In other words, the support service presents its work as primarily concerned with understanding and responding to Faupel's arena of 'interaction'. The delicate balance involved in establishing effective behaviour support cannot be underestimated. On the one hand there is the tendency for the behaviour support teacher to shy away from addressing school-related issues, leaving the professional development dimension of the service as a wishful afterthought, work that would be worth doing but that is too sensitive to pursue. On the other hand, there is the danger of shifting so much into developmental work that teachers feel their concerns about behaviour are discounted and that there is an over-reliance on the infallibility of the school effectiveness model. This is a possibility recognised by Watkins and Wagner who cite the work of Gottfredsons:

> Research implies that misbehaviour in schools has determinants at three levels:
>
> (a) some individuals are more likely than others to misbehave
> (b) some teachers are more likely than others to produce higher levels of misconduct in their classroom by their management and organisational practices
> (c) some schools more often than others fail to control student behaviour.
>
> Behaviour change programmes that reduce risk for misbehaviour at all three of these levels are most likely to be effective.   (Watkins and Wagner 2000)

Really successful behaviour support is based on the premise that a rich mix of factors make for problem situations and subsequent solutions. Consequently, it should be anticipated that intervention operates at different levels, and often at the same time! By delivering interventions that are isolated from other points of engagement, behaviour support teams can inadvertently sustain patterns of problem behaviour.

Case study: From theory to operation

This extended description is a composite from across services currently using the three-tiered model. These services are based in inner city, suburban and county LEAs or, to a modified degree, in schools through on-site provision.

The service has a clear aim to increase the inclusive capacity of schools. Its three objectives reflect the three tiers of intervention:

- To provide advice, understanding and support in developing whole-school responses to and the promotion of behaviour.
- To provide support to individuals or groups of professionals to increase their confidence and competence in dealing with problem behaviour.
- To provide a holistic approach to meeting the needs of individuals and groups of pupils.

While the objectives are linked to specific types of interventions the service works on the assumption that there is an inter-linking across the three key aspects: whole-school-adult-child dynamic. Any change in one of the areas will have an impact on the others.

Reflecting collaborative practice in service delivery

Not surprisingly the service is multidisciplinary both in terms of its professional composition but also in how it integrates with other local services and statutory agencies. The service regards itself as a catalyst for multi-agency intervention, either delivering it directly through the team or brokering partnership with other agencies. The services include youth workers, play workers, teacher assistants, social workers, educational psychologists and education welfare officers in addition to teachers. The role of each professional is carefully drafted to ensure compatibility with other team members while also reflecting the distinctive contribution that each discipline brings to behaviour support.

Due to the multi-professional nature of the team, where the service works across local schools (as opposed to being based in a single school), the team does not operate on a patch system. There are a total of 12 full-time members of staff in addition to sessional input from specialist teams, for example educational psychologists.

There is no predetermined allocation of hours per school or attached support worker for a given school. In one suburban LEA the multidisciplinary team had extensive links to other agencies, some with specific contracts involving sessional input to the service, for example the youth offender team, local education business partnership, traveller service and mental health voluntary service. Given an underlying belief that problem behaviour can be shifted through multi-professional intervention it follows that no one team member will have a monopoly on solutions. Consequently, allocation of work to projects and individual cases falls to the team member most appropriately skilled to deliver an efficient and effective way forward.

In operational terms this creates a managerial headache – the neatness of the allocated patch system whereby individual team members self-manage casework from a group of schools does not exist in these services. Instead the approach is to best meet the demands of the clients, be they pupils, teachers or whole schools. This in turn raises the issue of team supervision, an area of peripatetic practice that has long demanded review. The implication of shifting away from an allocated, patch system is that far greater levels of casework monitoring and staff support are necessary. The benefits in these services are:

- There is greater potential for projects to be linked to other activities being delivered via the support service in the same school and thereby maximising resourcing. For example in one school there were three interventions being run at the same time:
  - group work with Year 9 pupils focusing on developing social skills as a result of increasing concerns from tutors;
  - providing fortnightly problem-solving sessions for staff using the collaborative approach developed by Gerda Hanko (see Hanko 1999);
  - casework for four pupils for whom group work was not appropriate and who were all at risk of permanent exclusion.
- Projects can be allocated to the workers with the most appropriate skills. For example, a teacher might lead group work but a youth worker provides additional input. Equally other agency input can be bolted onto a behaviour support service project, for example through utilising mental health specialist input to transition project work (see case study material on multi-agency work in Chapter 3).

There are other advantages for services in dispensing with the patch system, since schools are not able to be possessive about individual team members. This often leads to a tendency on behalf of schools to develop a sense of the behaviour support teacher as expert, the person who has the answers. Conversely, this arrangement can leave the school exasperated that the support worker appears to be successful only in particular circumstances and not in others. On the other hand the allocated support teacher can become too closely associated with the school and eventually find it difficult to maintain a critical perspective on school culture and practice. In the worst scenarios the support teacher becomes an apologist for the school and defends practice that inhibits healthy development.

The strength of an effective behaviour support service lies in its diversity, either as a result of the team composition and/or due to its networking capacity. The conventional allocation of casework limits this crucial dimension.

Marking time – missing the point

Another important factor that marks out effective behaviour support relates to the spurious practice of delegating time to schools. I have never been convinced of the efficacy of this practice of doling out support time, particularly in relation to the volatile world of behaviour support. The convention of delegated time has been associated with budget delegation, which has been popular in a number of LEAs at different stages over the last decade. However, the business of setting up arrangements for delegating service time can be highly damaging and should be avoided and certainly not invited by services. The reason for this resistance is simple enough: it denotes a preoccupation with *input*. Effective behaviour support is essentially focused on outcomes. What do we want to happen as a result of the support? This is the question that should inform discussions and eventually lead to consideration of the level of resources required.

In most of the services using this three-tiered model it would not be uncommon to find three or four team members working in a single school on a combination of project and casework. Equally it would be the case that while a school might be supported during the spring term, there might be little if any input during the following term. For instance, a school requesting training for midday supervisors wanted the sessions in the spring term in preparation for the summer months and had no other need for development support for the rest of the year. The resources of the service are deployed to best meet the varying range of work across a number of schools at the most appropriate time.

Being clear about casework

In all of the services partnership planning is used as the model for negotiation and this process is covered in greater detail in the following section. In general the work of the service falls into two types: project work and individual casework. Individual casework is about support for a pupil who has been taken on for direct work, which could include a combination of the following:

- in-class support, either by teacher, teacher assistant or youth worker;
- support through withdrawal;
- family work;
- contributing to special educational needs assessment.

Any other service activity is referred to as project work which might include:

- group work for pupils;
- team teaching;
- lesson observation;
- whole-school development activities;
- training for learning support assistants (LSAs), middle managers, pastoral team, governors, midday supervisors etc.;
- problem solving for staff.

Providing effective support works on the assumption that defining the focus for intervention can take time and partnership. In these services there is no sense of referral in the conventional sense. Instead intervention is determined through negotiation not a referral form. Work in schools can be triggered by a number of routes:

- direct from the school via telephone or initial meeting;
- as a result of reviewing existing work with the school;
- on the recommendation of another agency, for example education welfare or inspector;
- on the recommendation of the LEA due to concerns about performance;
- as a result of parental concerns about their child's circumstances;
- via regular consultation sessions between behaviour support teacher (BST) and school link.

This last route – regular consultation – has proved to be a highly valuable way in which services have effectively marshalled the allocation of support. In one service this link was via the SENCO and was known locally as 'SENCO support' work. Another example is provided below.

Case study: A behaviour coordinator network

In an outer London LEA the primary behaviour support service, using the three tiered approach, developed a behaviour coordinator network with local schools. A member of staff from each school was identified, all of whom were from the school leadership team so were either head teacher, deputy head teacher, SENCO or senior teacher. Additional training was provided for the group by the behaviour service with the intention that these members of staff would be the channel through which all work by the service would be planned with the school. Regular consultation sessions were set up and this time was used to:

- monitor the progress of existing casework, both project and individual;
- identify emerging areas for intervention where appropriate.

In these schools, the need for referral forms and initial assessment was negated. Through individual supervision from the team leader new work would be identified and allocated to the most appropriate team member who was often not the person staffing the consultation sessions. Where schools did not have a behaviour coordinator the service would arrange a consultation session with a member of the leadership team to establish a sense of partnership prior to taking on any direct work. In potentially heavy user schools an initial objective would be to set up a behaviour coordinator system.

Getting the message across: convincing schools

One of the greatest challenges for moving into a systemic model of delivery is for the service to establish this identity within the local network, be it within a school or an LEA. The experience of services utilising this approach tells us that the conventional child-focused model of support is deeply ingrained in the mindset of schools, agencies and LEA officers, and not without reason. Many services running alongside the behaviour support service in schools will operate the conventional child-based referral-assessment-support cycle, so why would behaviour support be any different?

Educating other parties about the difference in approach can take time and is best achieved through generating local real-life casework as soon as possible. If the experience of schools has been to identify pupils in need as a route to secure external intervention, and if this had tended to be the sole focus of other services' input, it can be difficult to envisage how else support might look. Consequently an early task for the behaviour support team is to establish in the minds of schools that they do not need to have a list of troubled pupils in order to generate intervention. This is the key to the promotional strategy of the service. The prime message from the behaviour support service needs to be:

- This service is about schools becoming even better places for children and adults to work and grow.
- This service is about supporting adults to further develop their confidence and competence in working with children.

The service needs to generate messages that immediately reflect the objectives, aims and values that underpin this systemic model. However, care needs to be taken to avoid giving too strong a message about not working with children and families. Many services based on a systemic model *do* work with children but the emphasis is on systems-related support. In fact it is important that services do retain a level of work with children as they bring a critically important perspective to the design of intervention, in addition to maintaining credibility for the service in the eyes of mainstream teachers.

In several cases services using a systemic approach have worked quickly to provide a service 'brochure' presenting the full range of support available. In one example the document was colour-coded, with green pages at the front covering whole-school-based intervention, an amber section describing team teaching and group work and finally a red-paged section giving an account of individual work with children and families. Each section provided descriptions of the work offered and more importantly accounts by local schools of their experience of project work – including photos! The intention of the service was made clear in the presentation and content of the document. Furthermore, no referral forms were included, the partnership planning process was outlined and schools were encouraged to give the service a call to initiate work.

There are two other avenues that these services have found useful in spreading their alternative message:

- Establishing a service steering group incorporating membership from within the LEA, schools and other agencies. This can be an extension of the LEA's Behaviour Support Plan working group or other relevant existing committee. The advantage of this arrangement for LEA services – as

opposed to outreach or in-school services – is that in the absence of a governing body, the steering group members can be encouraged to take on the strategic planning and 'critical friend' roles provided by governors.
- Dissemination of monitoring and evaluation data, at least on an annual basis to validate working practice and legitimise service developments. The importance of this strategy cannot be underestimated; by sharing local experiences the service succeeds both in reminding colleagues that there is success and in raising awareness about the impact of alternative systemic support.

Local workshops and conferences have also been used in which the behaviour support service coordinates a central training event which enables local schools to present successful project work, once again establishing the service as a facilitator for mainstream achievement. These can also be valuable for drawing in less enthusiastic schools which are wary of the impact of outside agencies.

Getting the message across closer to home

Schools will understandably have reservations about alternative models of service delivery but we should not assume that these approaches will be necessarily understood by colleagues closer to home, including those from other agencies or key LEA officers. Some of the greatest resistance about systemic approaches experienced by behaviour support services team leaders has come from within LEAs, and once again not without good reason.

For many years in many authorities the role of the behaviour support team has been to provide a behaviour version of what many old-style learning support services have operated: individually focused direct support to pupils, with a limited level of class-based support. This work has often been tied in to local arrangements regarding pupils with special needs or reintegration plans for excluded pupils. In several instances the support team is directly led by the educational psychology service, and/or is based within the LEA's special educational needs/welfare division.

While the focus of behaviour support remains within the established conventions of pupil-based intervention, the role of the service fits well within the status quo. However, once the behaviour support team begins to see itself as an agent of institutional change, this has a knock-on effect for other services, in true systemic fashion – tinker with one element in the system and others are bound to change! I have come across a number of issues raised by support team leaders about the developing role of their teams. There appear to be two main themes that emerge:

- While members of other agencies and LEA officers are enthusiastic about the whole-school development aspirations of the service, they find it difficult to reconcile this when it comes to implementation. For example, a SEN assessment team continues to encourage referral of individual pupils

for support regardless of the consultative approach being used by the support service. An educational psychologist persists in making referrals for individual support on behalf of a school, without prior discussion, fearing that the school staff will not support the referral!
- More specifically, as the service makes more solid progress in addressing school-wide issues so it brings the work much closer into line with school improvement work. It is at this point that a new area of potential tension is exposed – the territory of the advisory and inspection service. In a number of cases the capacity for behaviour support to be available to schools in difficulty and to carry out remedial work at an organisational level has been greater than that of local advisor/inspector teams. Clearly this has implications for an inspectorate service that has a remit to monitor the performance of schools and intervene where need is greatest. This is an issue covered in more detail below but it highlights the importance of marketing a systemic model of behaviour support sensitively within the LEA as well as with schools.

The cautionary note for behaviour team managers in developing a systemic model is that the 'rules' for system change apply to the service as well as other partners! Few will take issue with the broad aims of the service but the chief task is to ensure that other teams understand what this means for them. Experience indicates that systemic behaviour support results in a highly mobile, adaptable and proactive local resource. For partners who feel 'stuck' in statutory assessment casework or entrenched working practices, the systemic behaviour support service can generate anxiety, anger and even a degree of envy. These feelings require sensitive consideration when planning the development of systems-focused behaviour support.

Behaviour support and school improvement

If it is not already clear by now, my own view is that effective behaviour support is inextricably linked with the school improvement movement. There is rarely anything that a support service is involved in that does not throw further light on how schools operate and their potential for realising the achievement of teachers and pupils. Historically behaviour support work has been firmly tucked into the world of SEN, which in turn has suffered for many years dislocated from mainstream school improvement debates. This has been to the detriment of the work of dozens of services which have struggled to forge a connection between how children behave and what and how schools choose to deliver to them. For too long there has been an unhelpful distinction between *teaching and learning* from *behaviour*. Best practice in behaviour support is about weaving together these three central dimensions; how schools deliver what they have chosen to deliver determines what they get back in terms of both achievement and behaviour.

Once again the emphasis on school improvement should not imply a negation of what pupils bring to the school arena. How schools respond to pupil needs and challenges can tell us a great deal about their values, policies and practice which in turn can be valuable information for LEA inspector services charged with the task of monitoring school performance. Consequently effective behaviour support is not just about developing school performance; for those services centrally operated by the LEA, contributing to local arrangements for monitoring school performance becomes a necessary and legitimate function of behaviour support. If behaviour support professionals are seriously interested in making connections between behaviour and teaching and learning, then establishing a genuine partnership with inspector and advisory teams is vital. From experience we know that this can be as challenging for behaviour support specialists as it may be for other professionals – it is, however, a non-negotiable factor for delivering successful behaviour support.

An increasingly familiar experience for LEA services is for their team members to be deployed into schools that have been identified as poorly performing. Team leaders are requested to free up staff and have them take on group work or staff development work, or simply increase the level of individual referrals in a particular school. It is a growing trend and one that reflects the pressure on LEAs to demonstrate that they are deploying resources where there is greatest need. Personally I suspect that this will significantly impact on how LEA behaviour support will develop over the coming years. In some areas the behaviour support teams have already begun exploring this territory and some early observations can be made.

- First, the behaviour support team would do well to ask how the presenting needs have been identified and by whom. A key consideration must be the extent to which the school itself and any targeted staff are aware that they have been identified. Team managers are strongly urged to check out these pre-planning considerations before engaging the school. A related question is whether any negotiation has already taken place on behalf of the support service by a third party. These queries may seem superfluous, but anecdotal evidence indicates that LEA officers, when endeavouring to resolve complex situations with schools in difficulties, can pull together 'solutions' without first checking resource implications.
- Second, the work of the behaviour support team in schools that have been identified as poorly performing should be part of a strategic plan for supporting the school. Poorly performing schools are rarely in difficulty because of behaviour issues – invariably high levels of problem behaviour are symptomatic of more fundamental issues to do with planning, staffing, leadership and governance. Consequently, simply throwing in more behaviour support to sort out naughty pupils is unlikely to improve the situation and may damage the reputation of the support service in the process.

  If the LEA has concerns about a school's performance then it needs to address underlying causal factors. This often involves supporting leadership teams, providing specific curricular advice and administrative support regarding finance and personnel. Any intervention from the service needs to be framed within the wider context of the LEA's response to the school's needs. Team leaders should be clear about how the work of their team accords with what other teams might be contributing.

On one hand this is difficult and challenging territory for behaviour support teams. I also believe that it is pioneering territory which a few services are now beginning to tentatively explore. The newness of this area of work is also reflected in the relative inexperience of inspectors and advisors in crossing boundaries. The line separating the broad beam of school effectiveness work and the nether world of behaviour support and provision for pupils out of school has for too long limited the sights of respective professionals.

Case study: Jumping into the void

A London LEA began introducing a framework for monitoring school performance in the mid-1990s, well in advance of many LEAs. The local inspectorate service worked with head teachers in devising an annual review of individual school performance which integrated school-based evaluation and external assessment. As the model became established a grading system was introduced which was intended to highlight those schools where additional support was needed and where effective management and practice was taking place. More recently the approach has been used to target additional support to those schools identified as having difficulties. The review tool used by both the school and the inspectorate for the external assessment included identical features of school performance and also included academic attainment, financial management, school leadership, personnel etc.

Initially the whole process involved only the schools and the inspectorate service – no other LEA personnel were involved. However, as the profile and status of the review process became more apparent, so it became increasingly necessary for other LEA officers and team managers to be involved. Given that the list of performance factors included pupil behaviour and attitude, special educational needs, community links and attendance, it became equally important that the behaviour support service also had input. The behaviour support team leader became a member of the LEA review meetings and contributed a range of data drawn from its involvement with a particular school. This included:

- the level of individual referral work as compared to similar schools;
- the level and range of projects taking place and how this compared with the take-up of other schools;
- issues regarding the management of pastoral care and in particular problem behaviour;
- perceptions of school staff and pupils drawn from group work and team teaching.

An extension of this work was to begin thinking about how school performance might be assessed in relation to behaviour to help identify those schools which, in relation to others, required additional support. At this point it became clear that behaviour support was entering into a new domain. The support service crossed the line that had separated school improvement from special educational needs. In effect this began shaping something that was approaching a more authentic sense of what social inclusion might mean.

Members of the behaviour support team expressed a number of concerns about entering into the school performance monitoring process. Objections included the following:

- The role of the behaviour support teacher would be irrevocably changed – some members felt that they were a critical friend of the school and that if they were seen purely as a stool pigeon for the LEA then this would contaminate their working relationship.
- Others were anxious about how information provided by the service might be used and possibly misconstrued.

These were legitimate concerns but they should also be put alongside other comments which members of the support service had raised in the past, such as:

- 'Why doesn't the inspectorate service do anything about supporting that head teacher? S/he is completely isolated by the leadership team and can't make much-needed progress.'
- 'The Key Stage 4 curriculum in that school desperately needs developing. The kids can't cope with the current curriculum options arrangement.'
- 'What are the inspectors doing about school X? It is really going to suffer when OFSTED visits next term.'
- 'All of Key Stage 2 are now being taught by supply teachers – is anyone looking at helping the school sort this out?'
- 'That school is a time bomb waiting to go off...'

Clearly the behaviour support team were picking up on wider issues about school performance and yet had no formal or systematic route through which to either raise concerns or become aware of what action might already have been taken. The local strategy for reviewing the performance of schools offered an obvious channel through which these queries might be addressed. Nevertheless there remained the tension for members of the team regarding their relationship with schools. A solution was devised that reminded the support team about its role within the LEA, in addition to safeguarding the relationship of individual team members with schools.

As a centrally maintained LEA service it was not unreasonable for the LEA to require the support service to contribute to the monitoring process. The intention was that the behaviour service input would be increasingly channelled to schools in difficulty and therefore more closely associated with the LEA's task of improving school standards. Therefore it was highly desirable for the service to be actively involved in the business of determining where the support might be targeted.

To preserve the integrity of the team it was agreed that the information shared with other LEA colleagues would also be made known to the school – there would be no covert record keeping. This led to the service drafting a grading mechanism which could be used and shared with school staff so that there was a high level of transparency in how the service assessed performance in relation to behaviour.

The proposals were successful in winning the confidence of the behaviour support service in addition to demonstrating to other LEA officers that the service was serious in making the link between school improvement and behaviour support.

School improvement and the role of the Learning Support Unit

The challenge to broker the connection between behaviour with teaching and learning is one that is not confined to those professionals working in LEA support services. Around the country many schools have been encouraged to develop Learning Support Units (LSUs) or similar on-site provision. The tendency has been for these initiatives to concentrate on providing education programmes for target groups of pupils. However, in some cases the development of the LSU is being seen as an opportunity to innovate how behaviour support is delivered from within the school.

For those staff working within the LSU provision the general trend has been for them to be deployed in working with groups or individual pupils. The focus is on changing behaviour and reducing exclusions. In some instances this has involved developing alternative curriculum options, experiential learning opportunities, and specialist input from counsellors and therapists. All of these features are typical of a sound, conventional behaviour support service. So, for example, in one inner city school the LSU operates as an internal multi-agency hub through which a wide range of individual programmes are tailored to meet needs and are met by contributions from particular specialist teams. Some of the input is made direct from a school-based professional, for example a social worker, or via an external service. The LSU serves a wide range of pupils including school phobics, those with emotional and behavioural needs and low achievers. However, the children are not brought together into a single group or venue.

Some schools have made a more determined effort to establish a systemic model of behaviour support. Consequently the activities of the LSU may (or may not) include a high level of work with pupils. Instead the LSU team are targeted more on supporting teachers through team teaching, professional development and mentoring. Another important dimension of this approach has been for the LSU to provide a monitoring system for picking up on patterns in whole-school behaviour with the result that curriculum, timetabling and organisational themes can be identified for further development. Needless to say, as colleagues more closely aligned with pupil-based issues begin to raise issues about whole-school and professional development issues, so resistance can build up among those for whom monitoring school performance has been the key role. Many of the dilemmas encountered by behaviour support specialists in LEA services (in building partnerships with curriculum advisors and inspectors) can also be reflected in school-based behaviour specialists' relationships with departmental/faculty managers.

Setting up system-based behaviour support: building the team and professional development issues

It is assumed that readers will be familiar with general approaches to team building, leadership and management. A useful source for more detailed consideration about developing the role of the leader and team development in the context of education support services is provided by Lacey and Lomas (1993). This section takes up these themes with particular regard to setting up systemic behaviour support teams.

The difficulties of recruitment and retention of mainstream teaching staff has been well documented in the national media for the past year. What has been given less coverage has been the particular difficulties in staffing suffered by many support services over the past two years. In part this has been due to the general trend in low recruitment, but for support services this has been compounded by national policies that have made it less attractive for experienced teachers to work in peripatetic services, especially those dealing with behaviour. The initiatives triggered by both the Excellence in Cities and broader social inclusion programmes, including introduction of school-based specialists, mentors and on-site units have resulted in staff in LEA services and outreach teams being 'poached' by local schools. The additional pressure felt by many LEAs to either delegate or disband support services has also meant that existing vacancies are vulnerable and offer little security to teachers, compared with being on the payroll of a school.

Another equally important dimension to recruitment, which affects staffing of behaviour support teams regardless of whether they are based in school, outreach or in an LEA service, is the task of getting the right person for the job. Obviously this is the case in any field of education, and when it comes to recruiting to a systemic-based team there are particular points to consider.

A common tendency when thinking about suitable candidates for delivering behaviour support is to seek out teachers who are known to be successful in working with disaffected pupils and/or those with emotional and behavioural difficulties. Not surprisingly staff already working in specialist provision are considered likely candidates. However, if the service is to operate systemically it is worthwhile considering the following scenario.

Case study: A case of mistaken identity

A school in an inner city area with approximately 1,500 pupils on roll and a low level of exclusions for the locality was in the process of setting up an LSU. Understandably the management team were keen to appoint a unit coordinator as soon as possible and were pleased to recruit a teacher from a special school for pupils with emotional and behavioural difficulties. However, during their planning for the on-site provision the school developed a model that focused predominantly on curriculum improvement, staff support and multi-agency intervention. It was agreed that the LSU would significantly limit the level of individual work undertaken. Shortly after the coordinator took up the post it became apparent that there was a mismatch between the competency of the member of staff and the more developed requirements of the LSU.

This scenario can also be replicated in LEA support services where teachers who are recruited purely on the basis of their capacity to work well with children are appointed to posts that demand a high level of skill in working with other teachers. Effective peripatetic work is dependent on staff being able to work extremely well with school staff in the first instance. Systemic behaviour work has arguably more in common with teacher training and advisory work in the sense that a high-level awareness about context is imperative. These observations should not be taken as a criticism of staff working within the specialist sector but it is important to point out that skillful systemic work is as much to be found among good mainstream practitioners as anywhere else.

Another important observation is that when setting up a systemic behaviour service it is worth remembering that teams tend to do what feeds their needs, aspirations and commitment. In other words, if a team has an underlying passion for helping poor, misunderstood youngsters by rescuing them from the horrors of brutal schools, then this can feed into the culture and practice of the service. In this instance it can become difficult to engender systemic practice; instead the team take on rescuing roles with all the clatter of charging knights in armour.

The key is to address team direction and service culture at the very first stages of recruitment. Job descriptions are all-important and need to reflect the range and emphasis of casework, making explicit reference to team teaching, policy development and group work as dominant aspects of the job.

The selection process needs to encourage candidates to consider how they might tackle systemic issues around organisational change. It is also worthwhile assessing individuals' teacher training abilities through mock presentations. Any in-tray or case study exercises should also reflect challenges about organisational issues. Finally, it is important to check with candidates that they understand that one of the implications of systemic behaviour support is that the level of direct work with children may not be as great as they anticipate. Staff inappropriately hanging onto cases can become a significant issue for team managers and one that can be partly addressed before they even have a job on the team.

The recruitment of non-teacher professionals can be equally difficult and the guidance for teacher recruitment applies to these posts, and perhaps even greater consideration needs to be given to defining their tasks. For instance, if behaviour support assistants are to be recruited care needs to be taken in how the job description for these posts correlates with those for school-based teacher assistants. On the basis of some experience services have found that where this has not been made clear – and where this ambiguity is reflected in partnership planning – schools have endeavoured to deploy specialist assistants no differently than other assistants. Once again the difference should be made clear in the initial job description – do not rely on existing mainstream personnel practice. An example of duties for a behaviour support assistant is provided in Figure 1.1.

Recruiting youth workers and home-school workers can also cause particular problems for team managers. Once again job descriptions need to make a distinction between the behaviour support posts and those in the mainstream youth service and education welfare service. If the behaviour support service does not make this distinction, it will become difficult for schools, other agencies and even the members of staff themselves to determine the purpose of their role. Examples of these job descriptions are included in Figure 1.2. For further discussion of the role of youth workers in schools, John Huskins' work provides extremely useful material regarding management and practice issues (Huskins 1999).

Duties

- Provide direct support to pupil within and outside of the classroom including:
  - making observations;
  - supporting pupil(s) developing learning/social skills through modelling tasks, encouraging successes;
  - arranging for set work to be more accessible for the pupil;
  - working with groups of pupils within the classroom;
  - working with the class teacher to reinforce positive behaviour and enforcing consequences.
- Contribute to reports for purposes of review and placement as required for individual pupils.
- Contribute to the work of the behaviour support team through attendance at meetings and participation in team activities and training.
- Attend joint home visits and liaise where appropriate with parents.
- Work sensitively within the context of individual classrooms.
- Liaise with other agencies regarding individual pupils where appropriate.
- Work in liaison with colleagues from other services.
- Attend team meetings.

Figure 1.1 Possible range of duties for Behaviour Support Assistants (drawn from material of existing posts)

The following descriptions have been taken from a range of existing descriptions from a range of services.

Job title: Youth Worker, Behaviour Support Service (BSS)

Responsible for: Providing a range of youth work interventions with teachers, parents and pupils

Main duties:

1. To contribute to the raising of school standards through the development of programmes that reflect the unique approach and methodology of a youth work curriculum.
2. To work as a member of the Behaviour Support Service to deliver innovative programmes to young people including individual and small group work.
3. To work closely with parents, carers, schools and local community groups.
4. To provide links between activities in school and local youth service provision.
5. To provide feedback to teachers on emerging concerns of young people.
6. To work with individual pupils outside of the classroom and where appropriate at venues beyond the school.
7. To support delivery of alternative curriculum programmes for target groups of pupils.
8. To provide mentoring support for individual pupils where appropriate.
9. To contribute to the development of constructive use of break and lunch-time periods.

Job title: Home-School Liaison Worker, Behaviour Support Service (BSS)

Responsible for: Providing a range of interventions with teachers, parents and pupils

Main duties:

1. To contribute to the raising of school standards through the development of activities that improve relations between children, families and schools.
2. To work as a member of the Behaviour Support Service to introduce strategies to improve attendance at school through whole-school policy and approach, group work and individual casework.
3. To work closely with parents/carers, schools and local community groups.
4. To enhance the existing involvement of the Education Welfare Service through extended work with specific families.
5. To provide feedback to teachers on emerging concerns of parents/carers and children.
6. To work within the context of the school and through home visiting.
7. To work in close collaboration with Education Welfare Officers and other outside agencies.

Figure 1.2 Job descriptions for Behaviour Support Team – Youth Worker and Home-School Liaison Worker

Building a team – sharing a vision

It is not the intention to provide here a detailed team-building programme. LEAs and schools will have local arrangements that will determine what is permissible in terms of time and resources. The following two exercises have been used with teams to generate discussion, provoke, challenge and ultimately to build a consensus about the purpose of the service.

Exercise 1: Establishing common aims and objectives

Divide the team into small groups or pairs. Provide each group with a set of the statements listed below. Ask the group to set out the statements in priority ranking using a diamond-nine format, i.e. first at the top, second and third in the second line, fourth, fifth and sixth in a middle line with seventh, eighth and ninth making up the lower half of the diamond.

Having completed the exercise each group feeds back their rationale for the ranking of statements.

Clearly the purpose of the exercise is to give team members an opportunity to increase their awareness of what behaviour support might entail. The range of responses will provide managers with a sense of where further thought needs to be given to expanding the remit of the team, while indicating areas of consensus. It is also a useful activity through which team members can share the values and assumptions that underpin their work.

- To raise attainment of pupils at risk of disaffection and poor achievement through individual support packages.
- To nurture and care for those pupils marginalised by school systems and/or family.
- To reintegrate pupils to mainstream who have been excluded.
- To reduce exclusions and truancy.
- To promote good practice in terms of teachers' behaviour management.
- To reduce the number of pupils with Statements.
- To reduce the need for emotional and behavioural difficulties (EBD) special school provision through specialist mainstream intervention.
- To support the development of whole-school policy and approach.
- To play a central role in establishing a local multi-agency strategy to promote social inclusion.

For colleagues developing support from an LSU base a similar exercise can be tackled using different statements. An example of what these might include is given below and is taken from *Learning Support Units: A practical guide to setting up and developing in-school provision* (Barrow *et al.* 2001a).

- The unit is essentially a way in which we can 'sort out' sad and bad kids.
- The on-site provision is an important resource for supporting staff development.
- Our in-school centre provides respite for children for whom school becomes too much at times.

- The unit is an extension of other forms of punishment which our school uses – it is well integrated within our approach to discipline.
- Our in-school service is aimed at providing preventative, in-class support to pupils and team teaching with staff.
- The unit provides us with a systematic approach to identifying pupils who should not be in mainstream school.
- The on-site provision serves as a hub for multi-agency input to our school.
- We provide pupils with a short-term programme that focuses on social skills and aims to modify their behaviour so they can be successfully reintegrated into classes.
- Our centre is essentially an office from which a range of support assistants, teachers and voluntary mentors go out to help students.
- The unit is all about reducing exclusion – fixed term and permanent.
- The unit is all about increasing our capacity to be an inclusive school.
  (Adapted from Barrow *et al.* 2001a)

Exercise 2: Who does what?

This exercise is intended for those services that have a multi-professional dimension, whether based in schools or an LEA service. A series of case studies is shared with small groups of team members representing each of the different professions, e.g. teacher, youth worker, support assistant. As with the first exercise, each group is given time to consider the cases and then contributes to a full team discussion. The purpose is to start to foster a team-based understanding of the potential contribution of respective members while also starting to determine professional boundaries. A possible team exercise for generating discussion about multi-professional approaches is presented in Figure 1.3.

Case study: Uncrossing lines – the importance of clear roles

In the early stages of a multidisciplinary support service, team members were extremely keen to be involved in as wide a range of activity as possible. After almost two terms difficulties began to emerge, with staff becoming unclear about their roles and responsibilities in relation to casework. Teachers who had been keen to develop playground games became uneasy about the role of youth workers linking with class teachers; behaviour support assistants voiced unease about leading class-based intervention, while youth workers became irritated at the perceived arrogance of some class teachers and the constraints of delivering youth work in the classroom.

Although the initial enthusiasm for interchangeable working arrangements had been well intentioned, in practice the notion that roles could be switched about threatened the team solidarity that it was meant to secure. By using similar material to the approach presented in Figure 1.3 it was possible to redefine the distinctive professional contributions within the team. It became important to establish a clearer demarcation of professional roles that in turn helped the team in recognising professional diversity – as opposed to homogeneity – as a strength. A handful of learning points from this experience are:

- Team managers should avoid the temptation to use staff interchangeably – even when invited to do so by individual team members.
- While the team may recognise significant commonality across professional approaches and consequently invite non-specialist deployment of casework, consideration must be given to the more conventional perception of schools and other agencies about the respective skill base and expertise of different professional groups.
- Team managers need to be explicit in communicating expectations of each professional type with regard to specific contractual terms and conditions, especially with regard to taking of leave.

Phase: ***Primary***

First thoughts:

- **What can each member of the group contribute to the following case in terms of experience, insights and training?**
- **What might each member seek to learn from others when delivering support?**

The school has identified a class which presents particular concerns. The class teacher shares the concerns of senior management and the SENCO. There are general worries about class management including noise, pupils wandering around the room, calling out and punctuality at the beginning of the day.

Most worrying is that there are two pupils in the class who are presenting more aggressive behaviour, picking on children and being abusive to staff. One of these pupils has already had a series of fixed-term exclusions and in both cases the parents feel helpless in managing their behaviour at home.

- What might be the key issues to address in this situation?
- How might the work be developed? Consider:
  - partnership planning and negotiation approach;
  - the time frame for the intervention;
  - the resources and approaches that might be used.
- How would the impact of the work be monitored and evaluated?
- What factors might potentially sabotage the intervention?
- Consider any multi-professional involvement factors:
  - Who from the team will be working on this casework?
  - What is the rationale for involving more than one type of professional input?
  - What will be their respective roles and responsibilities?
- If a situation similar to this case were in a secondary school, how might things be done differently?

Figure. 1.3 Material for multi-professional training exercise

Ongoing professional development

One of the key success factors in maintaining a systemic support team is securing an ongoing professional development programme for staff. A tendency can be for staff to be so busy delivering support and training other colleagues that the competency of team members can become jaded and taken for granted. Support staff need to continue to learn, reflect and think afresh about approaches to behaviour. The range of training and resources now available to mainstream staff is far greater than ten years ago and behaviour support specialists need to prioritise their own development.

Given that most schools have come across behavioural techniques, and given that those approaches tend to be most successful for working with groups of pupils and teachers on general behaviour management, it has been important to extend the skill base of behaviour specialists. Personally there have been three perspectives that I have found worthwhile in ensuring that the service remains ahead of the field.

Transactional analysis (TA) is based on a psychological framework of personal development and behaviour. It offers a theoretical model which I have found quickly engages teachers and provides a range of concepts that can be easily applied to the school context. Strategies for promoting emotional development, improving school culture, dealing with conflict and encouraging self-esteem can be rooted in psychodynamic theory and without the preconceptions that teachers can sometimes have about using therapeutic interventions. In one LEA service all team members attended a certificated introductory course in TA. The benefits of this included:

- establishing a common language for the team for discussing problem situations and understanding success;
- generating greater coherence in terms of service delivery;
- providing a standard 'entry-level' training dimension to the induction programme for new staff.

For further discussion of how TA can be used in the school context, see Barrow *et al.* (2001b).

Solution-focused brief therapy is another approach which offers a highly flexible range of techniques that are indispensable for the behaviour specialist. The approach is explored more fully in Chapter 3 when considering training for mainstream colleagues, but the work and literature of the London-based Brief Therapy Practice is highly recommended. The techniques can also be practised through in-house training, for example through a dedicated team meeting, and can give team members the opportunity to experiment and develop their in-service training skills.

Finally, the **ecosystemic perspective** has also offered some very alternative techniques for rethinking problem behaviour. Readers may be familiar with the work of Molnar and Lindquist, *Changing Problem Behaviour in Schools* (1989), which remains the core text for using ecosystemics in education. The capacity to re-frame problem behaviour and to positively connotate and respond to disruptive behaviour is a valuable skill for behaviour support teams and ecosystemic techniques are aimed solely at achieving this goal. There is little formal training offered in the UK in using ecosystemics, although several postgraduate courses on behaviour include sessions on the approach. For an account of how ecosystemic techniques have been used to train staff in Britain Ken Tyler's work with primary school teachers is recommended (see Tyler 1998).

Professional development does not always need to take the form of formal training. Having access to a well-stocked resource base is important and the systemic team library includes reference material on social work, welfare and curriculum development, in addition to the more obvious field of managing school behaviour. In addition, peer observation and paired work among team members can also be invaluable for increasing awareness, improving consistency and raising the quality of support.

2 Getting started

This chapter is about establishing effective behaviour support work in schools. It is divided into three parts:

- First is a consideration of contracting behaviour support work with schools. This includes a description of key principles for effective negotiation and presents a model called 'partnership planning' which has proven to be highly successful in setting up behaviour support intervention.
- A second section focuses on referral and assessment. This explores aspects of targeting systemic behaviour support by generating whole-school and professional development intervention through conventional pupil-based approaches.
- The final section offers some new ways of thinking about how behaviour support specialists can effectively engage with different school culture systems.

In my view the first stages in contracting, negotiation and action planning are the most important for ensuring best outcomes for behaviour support. In almost all my work the greatest successes are rooted in sound partnership planning and likewise, failure can be traced back to poor initial contracting. This chapter is arguably the most important in this book. If readers pick up only the ideas in the following chapter on practice, or take in the broad principles outlined in the previous chapter they will miss the catalytic ingredient which is the approach to initial planning. If there is one feature in the work of systemic behaviour support services that can make the key difference it is their use of the partnership planning approach.

Effective contracting

This section explores how negotiating behaviour support work with schools and teachers is the most crucial stage in delivering an excellent service. A number of issues about the limitations of conventional contracting arrangements are made and a well-tried model for establishing effective relationships between staff and pupils is described. The section covers similar ground to the chapter entitled 'Partnership Planning: Contracting in Schools', in *Improving Behaviour and Raising Self-Esteem in the Classroom*, by Barrow, Bradshaw and Newton (2001b). The difference here is that the focus is on the implications for contracting either as an external agency engaging with a school, or a support team from within the school. Different case studies are used and resources and exemplar material are specifically targeted at behaviour support work as opposed to more general school-based applications.

Conventional models for providing behaviour support tend to fall across a combination of the following arrangements:

- delegated support delivered from a central team;
- non-delegated support from a central team;
- outreach input from a specialist centre, e.g. PRU, special school.

More recently there have been other avenues through which behaviour support is being delivered:

- from particular types of on-site centres/LSUs;
- targeted input to schools identified as poorly performing as part of an LEA school improvement programme;
- support bought in directly by the school from the voluntary/private sector.

The emphasis in planning behaviour support tends to centre on the following themes:

- problem identification;
- negotiating input;
- allocating roles and responsibilities.

While these are important aspects of negotiation they do not tend to address the factors that are most often linked to partnership failure. To reduce the potential for difficulty the following issues also need to be addressed:

- identifying the purpose of the work;
- evaluation and monitoring arrangements;
- clarifying procedural/domestic details;
- predicting relapses;
- checking out whether partners have the professional competency and/or resources to take part effectively in the activity.

There is a subtle blend of factors that weave together to form effective behaviour support contracts between partners, and the complexity of the process can often be underestimated. In addition, short-cutting the planning invariably leads to frustration and inefficient use of time – both for the school and for the behaviour support service.

A number of services have been developing a model of contracting called partnership planning. First introduced in behaviour support during the early 1990s in Merton LEA (see Barrow 1998), the practice has now spread across teams around the country and is used by other types of support services. Support professionals have found that the planning approach significantly improves the possibility of establishing effective interventions with schools and minimises the potential for difficulty.

Partnership planning: first principles

Before we look at the operational aspects of partnership planning it is important to understand the principles that underpin the approach. The six key principles should be considered as a complete set – they are not offered as a 'pick 'n mix' choice where some are adhered to and others discarded. Within any contract some principles will be more pertinent than others, but all of them need to be addressed during the negotiation period.

Why are we having a contract? Identifying the importance of purpose, outcomes and agendas in contracting

When first negotiating behaviour support the tendency is for the contract to be regarded as two-dimensional, for example between the school SENCO and an individual behaviour support teacher. The emphasis is on determining the precise level of support to be delivered, often expressed in number of visits or sessions – in some areas this has even included the number of hours! Associated details might also include anticipated number of referred pupils and response times. These arrangements often focus on a description of a problem – almost always based on a child's difficulty – and conclude with a statement of how the service intends to resolve the situation for the school. In many cases there may also be reference to the role of the teacher and/or the parent/carer.

In the experience of this well-established approach to negotiating work, services have become increasingly aware of the critical business of referral and more adept at refining a standard patter regarding the negotiation of referral and service delivery. Behaviour support teams have recognised that providing a simple, accessible process can swiftly result in an overwhelming number of referrals; that waiting lists can be extremely difficult to manage; and that this can lead to poor-quality initial assessment and identification by schools. Inadvertently school staff are encouraged to shift the task of assessment, as well as intervention, elsewhere. In response some support teams have extended their referral pro forma to cover an increasing depth of assessment with the introduction of more lengthy and complex pro formas. Not surprisingly schools express frustration at what is perceived to be a stalling tactic and the delayed intervention has less chance of success due to deterioration in circumstances. Other frustrations that can be heard and that can be associated with the limitations of conventional contracts include:

- 'We have to wait ages for behaviour support by which time we have had to exclude the child.'
- 'That school always heaps the blame on kids – they cannot see how the attitude of teachers causes most of the problems.'
- 'The behaviour support teacher is really nice but their available time is so short that they can't make much difference.'
- 'The SEN department don't "do" behaviour – that's for Heads of Year.'
- 'The trouble in that school is that behaviour issues always fall to the pastoral team yet we know that the curriculum needs sorting out.'

- 'We wanted the Learning Support Unit to be a resource for staff, but we just don't have the time with all the referrals we've been getting.'
- 'If our school cannot hold a kid then no school will – the behaviour support team just does not understand this.'
- 'We had the team in and they did some work with a kid who was really difficult. They have closed the case but he's still not wearing the correct uniform or doing homework…'

Three-cornered contracting

In considering a different approach to contracting, one of the first stages is recognition that contracting operates not just at an explicit, formal level but can be used to understand what is going on under the surface of working practices. For instance, the focus of most negotiation of support tends to centre on the expectations of the service by the school – it is essentially a two-way contract. This type of contract is likely to have significant limitations; most importantly, effective contracting is seldom expressed in two dimensions because both the support teacher and school SENCO are subject to expectations made by the school and behaviour support service.

In other circumstances, for example where support is being provided by the on-site unit to mainstream staff, the third party might be the school. (For more detailed discussion of the contracting arrangements for colleagues working in on-site provision, see Barrow *et al.* 2001a.) From the perspective of outreach support, the third party might be the LEA but possibly the PRU or special school. The three-dimensional aspect to contracts is illustrated in Figure 2.1 and shows a range of possible scenarios.

Presenting the notion of a third party can be a highly useful mechanism for depersonalising contractual situations. We can refer to this as **three-cornered contracting** or **triangular contracting** and it is based on the work of English (1975). Often fourth and fifth parties can also be identified. By exposing the influence of what might be referred to as a 'Big Power' – which is rarely physically present during contracting negotiations – the parties can have more realistic hopes of establishing a sound contract. In effect this stage of contracting enables exposing powerful agendas with a view to setting up transparent arrangements for partners to work together.

Contracting negotiations that do not make explicit reference to the respective expectations on each of the parties are bound to fail. The reason is simple enough: the expectations of the third party are more often than not the driving force behind the parties having a contract. It is really important to see who is pulling strings behind the scenes. Individual teachers can often be unaware of the LEA's expectations of the behaviour support service to deliver a specific type of intervention, reduce exclusion, target staff development themes or other requirements set by the school.

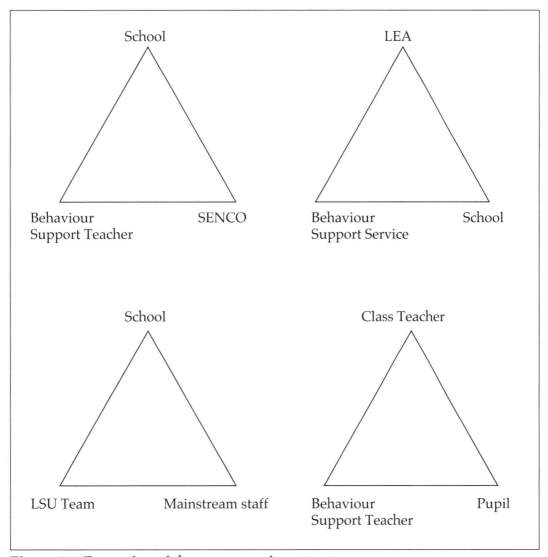

Figure 2.1 Examples of three-cornered contracts

Case study: Clarifying purpose through contracting

Let us look at an example in more detail. A behaviour support teacher is negotiating support in a large primary school where there has been an increase in fixed-term exclusions of Year 5 pupils. The school's performance is being reviewed by the local inspectorate team prior to a formal inspection and an important success indicator for the behaviour support service, set by the LEA, is a reduction in local exclusion rates.

At an early planning stage the behaviour support teacher and Head of Year (HOY) 5 are involved in detailed discussions about half a dozen individual children all of whom are in one tutor group. The HOY is primarily interested in sorting out the problems with the individual pupils; he does not want this minority group jeopardising the review and inspection process. The support teacher has a keen interest in preventing the use of exclusion and believes that there is a need to address issues about inconsistent management of pupil behaviour across the whole Year 5 tutor team.

Within a short time the HOY and behaviour support teacher are finding negotiation difficult; the HOY is becoming frustrated at the resistance of the service to take on the individual referrals while the support teacher feels under pressure to relent and agree to an inappropriate intervention. What can often happen as a form of temporary resolution is that either party gives ground and is drawn into work that is an unsatisfactory compromise. The school may be initially relieved that the service is taking on the recalcitrant pupils but then becomes disappointed when difficulties recur. The service becomes exasperated when the staff training input falls flat through lack of attendance and commitment.

It is clearly crucial for both parties to address a number of factors in building a deal that (a) will be sustainable and (b) is based on a win-win outcome. It is a challenging task; how might it be achieved? Before any discussion takes place about the contract between the support teacher and HOY, it is imperative that each party shares their relationship within the context of the school and LEA. In many respects, it is the combination of the demands on the HOY 5 by the school and those on the support teacher from the LEA that cause both parties concern. The requirements to reduce exclusions and establish stability for the review and inspection period are the prime concerns for the support teacher and HOY. The *purpose* of the contract is really important and is linked to wider expectations.

The targeted pupils will also have views of what the school expects, in terms of their behaviour, but also a more general sense of the purpose of being at school. Similarly the Year 5 tutor(s) will also have expectations about how the school might support them and likewise the school will have expectations of tutors in dealing with pupil behaviour. On the other side of the arrangement the behaviour support service will have expectations of its staff within the broader context of those of the LEA. It is important to establish what these expectations are at the outset because all parties need to eliminate any misunderstandings about what the others expect from the contract.

One of the most common fault-lines in negotiating behaviour support work is that there is insufficient transparency about why work is being planned in the first place. In Figure 2.2 there are some examples of activities listed, the purpose driving the work and possible misunderstandings, or fantasies, that might exist.

A development of the three-cornered contracting process is **psychological distance** and this can help us understand why partnerships sometimes get stuck. Based on the work of Micholt (1992), psychological distance refers to the collusive relationships that can develop in partnerships, often outside of the awareness of respective parties. As a result a pact between two partners can inadvertently be set up that can isolate or persecute the third party. An example of how this might take effect in behaviour support work is presented in Figure 2.3.

Activity	Purpose	Possible fantasies
Group work for disaffected boys at Key Stage 4	The group has been identified as most at risk of exclusion by pastoral team – the group work is intended to provide support to *sustain* their placements.	• The boys believe that they are continually being picked on by staff. • The boys understand that they are 'special', in preference to disaffected female pupils. • Staff are resentful that pupils are being rewarded for poor behaviour. • Staff believe that the group is the last chance for the pupils before being excluded. • The behaviour support teacher believes that the work should lead to improving staff attitudes.
Deploying behaviour support staff into a Year 2 class	The class teacher has been identified as having difficulties in planning and delivering core subject material. Several pupils are now falling behind.	• The class teacher believes that senior managers have now acknowledged that s/he has a very difficult class in terms of behaviour. • The class teacher believes that his/her lessons have been chosen to give the support teacher an opportunity to practise skills. • The support teacher believes the main task is to do 1:1 work with pupils, possibly using withdrawal from class.
Additional input for dealing with whole-school behaviour issues	A school has been identified by the LEA as having high exclusion rates and has encouraged the behaviour support service manager to increase available support for professional development.	• The school believes that additional support is to help with individual pupils. • Some staff understand that the support is to aid transfer of pupils into special school/unit places. • The support teacher works on the assumption that the staff lack sound behaviour management expertise.
Developing an in-school centre	Provide support to staff in developing successful approaches to managing behaviour with limited specific sessional input for target pupils.	• Mainstream teachers believe that the centre is essentially about respite for troubled pupils. • Targeted pupils assume that the alternative approach is a long-term option. • Centre staff assume that mainstream staff understand and accept the implications of the dual role of the provision.

Figure 2.2 Contracting: purpose and fantasies

Activity	Purpose	Possible fantasy	Collusive relationship
Deploying behaviour support teacher into a Year 2 class	The class teacher has been identified as having difficulties in planning and delivering core subject material. Several pupils are now falling behind.	• The class teacher (CT) believes that senior managers (SMT) have now acknowledged that s/he has a very difficult class (C) in terms of behaviour. • The class teacher believes that his/her lessons have been chosen by SMT to give the behaviour support teacher (BST) an opportunity to practise skills. • The support teacher believes the main task is to do 1:1 work with pupils using withdrawal from class so vulnerable pupils (P) are not further disadvantaged by the class teacher's poor teaching.	SMT ... C / CT (triangle) SMT ... BST / CT (triangle) CT with BST and P (triangle)

Figure 2.3 Psychological distancing in behaviour support work

Linked to the task of clarifying the purpose of the contract is the business of agreeing what the parties want as a result of the contracted activity. Skipping the discussion about purpose can result in a divergent notion of success for each partner. For instance, if a behaviour support teacher is being deployed into a class for particular sessions it is crucial for the class teacher, support teacher and pupils to be clear of the role of support, for instance is it to:

- generally support the teacher in the lesson;
- introduce a specific strategy through leading sessions;
- work with a specific group of pupils;
- work with a targeted pupil?

Only having clarified this aspect can colleagues then begin to identify whether this activity will have been successful. For example, if the support teacher's role is to lead on introducing a specific strategy this might be measured in terms of how effective the approach was in changing behaviour and the extent to which the class teacher was able to take on the approach. Whereas if the intention was to provide support to individual pupils the relative success of the partnership might be determined by factors regarding specific pupil progress.

Contracting behaviour support can tend to focus too much on describing what partners *must do* and less clarity around what parties *want to achieve* through working together – there can be an unhelpful preoccupation with *input*. Effective contracting involves 'front-loading' discussions with consideration about outcomes. One of the possible difficulties that can emerge in negotiating behaviour support is a sense of unease that colleagues have in exploring the wider context in which the contracted activity is taking place. For example, the period pre- and post-OFSTED inspection can raise a number of sensitive issues for schools and LEAs, resulting in a re-prioritising of tasks. Sometimes this leads to making changes in the role of staff or developing specific activities, for example a reorganisation of management, or a restructuring of local services. It might also involve targeting groups of pupils or members of staff where much needed development work is initiated. In all of these cases it would be necessary to refer explicitly to inspection action plans/preparation as the motivation for the work. Failing to do so can leave colleagues and pupils at liberty to fantasise about the purpose. Some questions worth asking at the earliest stage of planning include:

- Why is this work being developed now?
- How will we know if this has been successful?
- Who wants this work to happen?

Three-cornered contracting: some implications

In an ideal negotiation representatives from all parties should be present in order to contribute their respective expectations in terms of purpose and anticipated outcomes. However, this is often difficult to arrange, especially given the time constraints that many colleagues in schools face. Sometimes this can be overcome through a 'proxy representative', for example, where the position of the head teacher is relayed via the SENCO in a negotiation about support for particular children, or where the support teacher relays the perspective of the behaviour support service or line-managing LEA Officer. In the case of outreach work the support teacher may need to explicitly outline the PRU manager's/special school head teacher agenda. It is important to recognise that whenever a third party is absent, the possibility for misunderstanding is greater. This has particular implications for managers in terms of their feeling hijacked or misunderstood when a new project is not going in the direction they had intended. For complex pieces of work, for example policy development, targeted groupwork, interventions with other schools and agencies, it is advisable not to initiate project delivery until the lines of communication – including the deployment of any proxy representation – have been fully established.

'Which room have I got?' The importance of domestic details in contracting

Have you ever had the experience of turning up at a school to meet with a group of pupils only to find that the school was closed for staff training? Or that the child you were planning to work with is absent and no one let you know before you travelled across the county to work with him or her? Or the time when you had requested a quiet room where you could work discreetly with a particular group only to find that you had been allocated an area that operates as a corridor at lesson changes? How about the instance when the support teacher arrives to deliver a twilight training session on circle time for staff to discover that they have been given half an hour within a staff meeting. In all of these examples the behaviour support work is scuppered early on. Bad news does not just happen to behaviour support teachers. Schools express frustration at there being no cover arrangements for when support staff are ill, or when swift changes in allocated personnel are made with no explanation, or when unrealistic demands are made on teachers' time.

In negotiating with colleagues we can so easily forget the significance of *procedural* aspects – the domestic arrangements. Often this might be because of the familiarity partners have in working together or perhaps it is due to rushed planning when discussions focused too much on describing what appeared more important themes and less on the seemingly peripheral details about room availability or managing absence. Some procedural questions might be:

- Where will the work take place?
- When will the work take place? How often?
- What room/equipment/resources/copying will be needed? Who will ensure that these are arranged?
- Are there any funding implications for this work? Who will fund the activity?

In some instances misunderstandings regarding procedural details can be swiftly resolved. However, it is important to recognise that forgetting the apparent peripheral matters of partnership working can give some very powerful negative messages. This is invariably the case when there have been difficulties in agreeing the purpose for the activity or when there is a history of difficulty in previous work between the parties. Consider the following scenario.

Case study: The importance of procedural details

For months a PRU has been trying to establish outreach support to pupils at a local secondary school. There has been a perceived resistance by the school to accept support for a couple of pupils at risk of exclusion. The PRU staff believe that the school wants to secure a managed move for the target pupils. Arrangements are eventually put in place and sessions set up for the support worker to meet with the pupils. Careful attention is given to the subjects from which the pupils can be withdrawn for support and for the first half term the work progresses well. Then immediately after the half-term break the timetable for the year group is changed and the previous arrangements for the two pupils have clearly been forgotten.

In this example the procedural issues around attendance are as important as any other aspect of the contract. The forgetfulness of the school begins to fuel latent concerns of PRU staff that the secondary school does not want the outreach to succeed so that a managed move can be initiated. There are a number of consequences, one of which will be a greater degree of suspicion in any future planning between the parties. In drafting effective contracts colleagues ignore the procedural details at their peril.

Horses for courses: acknowledging competency in contracting negotiations

One of the reasons why partnerships can break down is that partners gradually realise during an activity that the expertise required lies outside of the competency of one or both partners. An example of this might be where the Learning Support Unit is contracted by the pastoral deputy to work with a group of Year 9 pupils on developing thinking skills. The deputy becomes exasperated that the LSU team is actually delivering sessions on anger management. Alternatively, the support teacher might assume that an experienced head of department has a working knowledge of behaviour theory and then become frustrated at recurrent difficulties regarding classroom management.

In both of these cases there may well have been agreement at the contract stage regarding the purpose of the activity, its wider context and *procedural* aspects. However, assumptions were made about the ability of each partner to deliver the contract and therefore problems were likely to emerge. Understandably, when asking questions about competency a high degree of tactfulness is required. Some questions worth asking to determine professional competency include:

• What expertise does the partner bring to the task? This is a useful question for managers to ask when building up a team profile, especially in multi-professional teams.
• How familiar are they with the context in which the work will take place? This is an especially important question to consider where non-teachers, for example social workers or youth workers, are being deployed to work in a

school. It is also an important consideration when deploying new members of the support team. Managers must make no assumptions that the new teacher will have a shared perspective on a particular school's context.

- What joint experience do we bring to this task?
- Where have partners worked on similar activities?

There will be many partnership arrangements where the clarification of competency is not a significant issue. Where colleagues have been working well together it may be safe to make assumptions about respective expertise.

Establishing the competencies of each partner at the outset will provide all parties with a degree of protection. No one should find themselves in a position where they feel vulnerable (due to being asked to do things they cannot do) or become frustrated (because basic arrangements have been forgotten which undermine the purpose of the work). An example of this might be where the team's youth worker is given the task of providing classroom management advice to a longstanding and cynical class teacher. While this might provide support teachers with a break, this in effect sets up both the youth worker and class teacher to fail – not enough consideration has been given to the protection of the partners by the 'Big Powers'.

Process, process, process

Inevitably contracting discussions tend to centre on the business of how colleagues intend to work together – the *process*. As has been commented on earlier, the tendency in behaviour support can be to focus too much on this aspect of contracting. It is nevertheless an important dimension. This should be done having already established the context of the work and its driving forces. Defining roles and responsibilities provides a more detailed picture of what project delivery will look like. It is the part of negotiation that enables colleagues to say what it is they will do and also what they will *not* be doing. It also allows for a more comprehensive discussion of procedural detail.

Questions worth asking relating to process aspects might include:

- How will we work together?
- Who will do what?
- Is there clarity over where different responsibilities lie?
- How will differing roles be made clear to other partners?

Providing for the relapse: addressing psychological aspects in contracting

For the most part, the experience of contracting will be one of players keen to get started on working together to achieve a common goal. During negotiations people will often be anxious to ensure that misunderstandings are clarified in order to avoid bad feelings and wasted time and effort. Colleagues work on an assumption that, given thorough planning, activities will be more likely to succeed. However, experience shows that often things go wrong; people fall ill, diaries become crowded, staff move on. A number of factors that fall outside the control of the contracted parties can shift the intended direction of the work.

In addition, there can be developments at a psychological level operating outside of the consciousness of individual players. These may not be evident at the outset of negotiation, or even during the early stages of activity. However, these psychological factors will tend to become a dominant feature during the development of the work. One way of illustrating this aspect of contracting is to return to the exemplar material in Figure 2.2. In each case there are potential fantasies in the minds of individual parties. One of the dangers might be that people begin to behave as if their fantasy about another's motivation is real. In other words, a teacher begins to project negative messages onto the behaviour support teacher about excluding pupils, despite having asserted that he or she wants the pupil to be at the school.

In effect, what happens is that individual players can find themselves inadvertently sabotaging contract agreements. The difficulty can be that this only becomes apparent after the work is well under way. By this point partners can be too angry or disappointed to be able to think about the situation in a helpful way. Consequently things get stuck and in some instances work is abandoned or gradually fades to closure. The longer-term impact of this deterioration on behaviour support should not be underestimated.

One of the most overlooked aspects of planning behaviour support in schools is providing for possible relapses. In our enthusiasm for ensuring that a partnership will work, support personnel can be reticent about considering how arrangements might be vulnerable to changed circumstances or shifting perceptions of the partners. It may appear a peculiar recommendation, but inviting partners to consider how arrangements might be undermined can prove a valuable part of the contracting exercise.

Take the example of a support teacher contracting with a group of pupils about a series of sessions aimed at increasing self-awareness. It will be important for the support teacher to raise with pupils the issue of how best to manage inappropriate behaviour if it occurs, with any suggested strategies needing to reflect the wider school approach. Likewise, in negotiating the role of a learning mentor it would be appropriate to consider at the outset how to avoid the possibility of colleagues leaving the mentor alone to deal with pupils' difficulties without support. Another common area worth addressing is the dissemination of project work at the end of the support period. A notorious difficulty for behaviour specialists can be in securing time and commitment for project follow-up, either through dissemination or by involving other staff. Often inadequate time is spent at the outset planning for this important aspect and consequently it can be regarded as unimportant by the end of the process. Relapses are entirely normal developments – in many situations they are also predictable: possible changes in staffing, illness, breakdown in behaviour. In contracting negotiations potential sabotage questions can include:

- How might partners find themselves undermining the contract?
- What could partners find themselves doing that sabotages the work?
- What is going on that might threaten success?

- What early warning system do we have to alert partners when things start going wrong?

Finally – *Physis* (Greek: meaning 'life-force' or 'growth')

A sixth aspect to consider when contracting is establishing how the planned work fits in with the wider growth of each of the partners, or *physis*. The motivation of colleagues is greater where an explicit link can be made with the development of the individual or organisation. For example, it might be important to locate the contracted introduction of circle time with a Year 3 class, within a broader school-wide initiative to raise self-esteem. Similarly, in improving a child's behaviour at school parents may be more highly motivated if this is linked to having better relationships at home.

In schools there can be a wide range of separately funded programmes involving an equally wide range of staff. The contracting process can be invaluable for generating discussion about how an individual activity fits within a programme of projects. Schools are increasingly encouraged to integrate activities in the school development plan and this is an obvious route for locating behaviour support work within the growth of the organisation.

Similarly it is important to identify at the planning stage where the work reflects the growth of the behaviour support team. If behaviour support managers cannot locate individual activities within the remit of the service it becomes difficult to justify resourcing or supervision commitment. All parties need an assurance that the work will help their respective developmental growth.

Some questions worth asking that encourage reflection of the *physis* dimension of the contract include:

- How does the work fit in with our work outside of this specific partnership?
- How will other colleagues understand this activity in relation to what they are doing?
- Are both partners able to identify 'what's in it for them'?

Contracting principles: summary

Schools have always been the forum for complex contractual situations, regardless of whether these are made explicit or remain at a hidden level. Whether partners are teachers, managers, other agencies, pupils or parents, contracting principles must apply in establishing effective, sustainable and successful relationships. A summary of the principles is presented in Figure 2.4.

Partnership planning: operational issues

Having a written contract is a common expectation when working in partnerships. In working with schools there is already a range of ways in which contracting takes place:

Contracting: underlying principles

Contracts may or may not be written down. A verbal contract is still a contract. The main point is that we discuss and agree why we are interacting as we work together. Contracts operate at different levels – all levels need to be clear to avoid unwitting sabotage.

The Six Contracting Principles

Procedural – administrative details, such as when colleagues meet, where, how often, who keeps notes, payment procedure and domestic arrangements, e.g. resources, copying, etc.

Professional – what do partners offer in terms of their professional role, what is it that colleagues need and is this within collective competency?

Purpose – why are the partners coming together, what do colleagues want to achieve, and how will they know when it has been attained?

Process – how do partners intend to arrive at their purpose? How will they work together?

Psychological – what might occur outside of partners' awareness? How might either of them sabotage the process?

Physis – how does the purpose fit within colleagues' overall growth and development – is this an appropriate pathway to pursue with them?

The Three Dimensional 'P's

Protection	– **procedural** establishes clarity and avoids misunderstandings – **professional** implies delivering within limits of competency
Permission	– **purpose** defines the rationale for working together and the anticipated outcomes for the work – **process** establishes agreement about roles and responsibilities
Potency	– **psychological** dimensions are made explicit – *physis* acknowledges the wider context in which partners can grow

(Adapted from Hay 1995)

Figure 2.4 Summary of contracting principles

- Individual Education Plans;
- Statements of Special Educational Needs;
- Pastoral Support Plans.

Each of these has an associated administration, invariably involving the completion of pro formas. For a number of LEAs and schools, behaviour support has been developed using the partnership planning approach. Figures 2.5 and 2.6 are examples of partnership plans used by support services for behaviour and travellers. Unlike conventional contract arrangements, partnership planning is a highly detailed contract that focuses on a tightly defined task, which could include any one of a range of situations including:

- working with parents;
- providing support to an individual pupil;
- establishing group work;
- mentoring class teachers;
- team teaching;
- supporting pastoral/SEN school managers;
- developing whole-school approaches;
- working with other agencies.

The task of recording the partnership planning sessions is more than simply administrative. Pro formas have been developed which ensure that the central contracting principles are addressed during negotiations. In other words, where colleagues use partnership planning pro formas they significantly minimise the potential for frustrated or misunderstood contracts.

The important point to remember with partnership planning is that the contract is a 'live' document. It is the reference point for the joint task; when there is potential confusion or lack of clarity on any aspect, the contract serves as an agreed statement of intent. It is equally important to recognise that the contract is live in the sense that it can be reviewed and changed at any time. While a date might be set to formally review the work, the contract can be referred to by any party at any time when one group is unhappy with how things are developing.

When practitioners are handed most types of pro forma the general response is a series of objections about the burden of paperwork and it is well established that there has been too much paper-chasing in education. However, the partnership planning pro forma is not just another referral planning document. It should be used as a way of recording discussions about the development of work. It is not a form that any party completes by itself but one that emerges through negotiation.

The partnership planning pro forma is also a crucial management tool. It can be used as the only means through which legitimate behaviour support work is delivered: no partnership plan = no intervention. There are significant advantages to using the pro forma in this way:

- It reduces the tendency for individual behaviour support teachers to generate their own casework either through wanting to further 'help' a school or through being ambushed into taking on referrals by school staff. This is a significant point where it is intended to move away from the patch system of allocating work.
- It provides an efficient and informative method for monitoring the progress of individual support teacher caseloads. Behaviour support managers can use plans to help refocus casework supervision and support case closure.
- It can be used in conjunction with case management records to systematically feed into the monitoring and evaluation process (discussed in Chapter 4).

Referral Date: End Date:	Number of hours: Number of visits:

SUTTON PRIMARY BEHAVIOUR SUPPORT TEAM
Partnership Plan

Project Title: — **School:**

School Representative/s: — **PBST Representative/s:**

Aims of the Project:

Details of work to be undertaken:

Start Date: — **Anticipated end date:** — **Review date:**

	Who will be involved?:	**Nature of the work to be undertaken:**
School		
PBST		
Other		

Practicalities

	Who will arrange?	**When?**	**Where?**
Liaison/Communication with other staff in school			
Liaison/Communication with parents			
Liaison with Other Agencies			
Room for work to take place			
Provision of Resources (detail)			
Other (specify)			

Signed: .... (School) ....(PBST) **Date:** ....

Figure 2.5 A sample behaviour partnership plan

Referral Date: Number of hours:
End Date: Number of visits:

Notes from Review/s of Project: **Review Date/s:**

(Is a new Partnership Plan needed?)

Final Review   **Date:**

Evaluation against original agreed success criteria: **Comments on outcomes:**
School:

PBST:

Others:

GAS Marks (Goal Attainment Scaling) to be entered on Referral Form/s

	Intended	Achieved	GAS Mark (1 = high, 4 = low)
Programme developed and introduced	☐	☐	☐
Measurable achievements: Self-esteem assessments	☐	☐	☐
On-task behaviour	☐	☐	☐
School/staff audit undertaken	☐	☐	☐
Staff involved enskilled	☐	☐	☐
Feedback to Headteacher/SMT/wider staff	☐	☐	☐
Change in future practice	☐	☐	☐
Pupil Response	☐	☐	☐
Additional criteria arising from Review (Specify)	☐	☐	☐

Signed: .... **(School)** .... **(PBST)** .... **(Other)**
Date:

Figure 2.5 continued

Sutton&Merton
Traveller Education Service
SCHOOL AND SERVICE PARTNERSHIP

Between:_____School, and Traveller Education Service

Period of Support: _____ Date:_____

Link staff member in school: _____

Main focus of support: (whole school development and / or named pupils)	
Purpose: (why is this work needed now?)	Outcomes: (What changes do we hope to see?)
Links to School Development Plan, OfSTED, EDP, other plans/policies: (How will this support fit in with other work being carried out in school?)	
How will we achieve this?	
Who needs to be involved? (name and role in project)	
TES visits (when will TES visit for support and planning, for how long, and where will the work take place?)	

Figure 2.6 A sample partnership plan for travellers

What could stop us achieving our purpose? What should happen then?

Record-keeping — how will records be shared? Will there be an end of project report?

Signed (school): _____ Title:_____

Signed (TES): _____ Title:_____

copies to:_____

REVIEW DATE:_____

Outcome achieved:

Future action from school:

Future action from TES:

How can we celebrate this work?

Priority for Support for Traveller pupils:

1. Highly mobile
2. Late start to, or little experience of school
3. Secondary-aged pupil
4. Age of Transfer to new school
5. Initial settling period at school
6. Sporadic attendance

You can contact your TES team member on:

It may be necessary, from time to time, for the TES to shift their focus of support to higher priority pupils arriving in the area. This will usually be for temporary periods. We apologise for any inconvenience this may cause, and anticipate only short term interruption to ongoing work within your school. Should this happen the link staff member will be informed by the TES. We would then ask for them to be responsible for communicating this to all involved in the project.

Figure 2.6 continued

• It reduces the extent to which support teachers are left without support to negotiate in difficult situations – the pro forma is robust in that it addresses all core principles.

This last point is especially important; the partnership planning pro forma system offers a structure through which complex and sometimes sensitive issues can be addressed with minimal danger of discussions becoming personalised. Exploring whether the work is being driven by the outcome of a recent inspection or because of an LEA agenda is treated as a routine part of project negotiation. Likewise, asking school staff to consider how the work might be jeopardised can be regarded as a standard part of the planning process.

Specific guidance for using partnership planning

Experience indicates that invariably it takes longer to plan and arrange a project than is anticipated. Although the initial suggestion for a project will lead to swift conclusions as to what the work might look like, it is crucial that the detail of work is considered, and this is often complex.

It is expected that the planning will take at least two meetings and, for complex work, will span a period of weeks. The more partners there are involved, the greater the potential for misunderstanding and miscommunication and consequently the need for more time.

The final draft of the plan cannot be completed without the direct involvement of the colleagues involved in actually delivering the work. This can mean drawing in class teachers, assistants, managers and support personnel at the earliest possible stage in planning. The longer these key players are left outside of discussions, the more likely it will be that the initial concept of the project will be misunderstood.

The final draft needs to be copied to all partners, even where they have been absent from more detailed discussions. This document will be the key paperwork for the support service case file.

Experience indicates that all sections of planning pro formas must be completed prior to starting the project. Each component is designed to minimise the potential for misunderstanding and ambiguity. Attention should be given to the main objectives of the project as opposed to the level of resource required; *outcomes*, not input, should be the overriding concern (which is different from acknowledging the importance of process). Issues regarding monitoring and evaluation are considered in a later section, but it should be noted at this point that a common pitfall is to cut too short the consideration of these themes at the planning stage.

Referral and assessment

This section is not about the referral and assessment of disruptive pupils. Instead a range of approaches are considered that are intended to help practitioners identify and assess aspects of the school-teacher-pupil dynamic that most need intervention. In other words, the strategies are aimed at helping readers in shifting from what is presented as a pupil-based difficulty into one that also takes into account and addresses class or school-based issues. This is an important emphasis to establish and one that can be tremendously challenging for both schools and behaviour support services.

A conventional approach to delivering support invariably hinges on some kind of referral process that identifies a pupil in difficulty. From that point on possible strategies are considered and a plan of action devised. The intervention may, or may not, include targeted professional development but will almost always focus on some type of pupil-based intervention. Without repeating earlier discussions about the limitations of this model, the referral and assessment techniques that behaviour support staff use are important for two reasons:

- The process should give a clear indication of the fundamental values and intentions of the service at the earliest possible stage.
- The process should allow for a wide range of possible points of entry for intervention.

I am working on the basis that behaviour can only be fully understood by considering the context in which it takes place. It follows then that practitioners require a method for referral and assessment that generates insights into the contextual factors that impact on individuals' behaviour. Conventional assessment tools have tended to fail in this respect. There are some useful materials that can be used to determine the specific difficulty of pupils, for example, the *Boxall Profile* (Bennathan and Boxall 1998) or the *Pre-School Behaviour Checklist* (McGuire and Richman 1988). However, these and most other assessment tools are primarily focused on determining the extent of child deficit.

There are few assessment tools on the market that can be used to generate a more systemic assessment of behaviour. In the absence of a choice of material, several support services use solution-focused brief therapy techniques and these are considered in the following chapter. The *Behaviour in Schools: Framework for Intervention* model developed by Birmingham LEA (Birmingham 1998) has also gained popularity and in particular its environmental checklist. This provides a comprehensive listing of possible contextual factors that are considered prior to any work with individual pupils. The approach is very much a school-based programme, overseen by a Behaviour Coordinator using a staged approach to problem identification and assessment.

An alternative approach that has been developed over a number of years is the Coping in Schools Scale (CISS) developed by Jane McSherry. Initially the approach was used for assessing the readiness of pupils for reintegration from specialist provision. More recently the CISS has been used by mainstream schools and in-school centres for assessing a broad range of pupil needs and targeting behaviour plans. (For further commentary and details of the assessment tool, see McSherry 2001.)

Perhaps the most powerful assessment tool for use by behaviour support practitioners is the *Towards Better Behaviour* model developed by Mark Jolly and Eddie McNamara (1991; 1992). Many support services have used this material as the basis for identification and assessment and it has much to commend it from the perspective of the behaviour support specialist.

Using *Towards Better Behaviour* (*TBB*) for planning systemic intervention

The *TBB* resource is divided across three distinct parts: the Behaviour Survey Checklist, Assessment and Contracting. For the purposes of this book, the first two parts provide the most useful material for behaviour support services. The theoretical roots of the approach are the behavioural perspective but through careful use of the resources one can generate significant opportunities to deliver systemic behaviour support.

Using the Behaviour Survey Checklist

The Behaviour Survey Checklist (Jolly and McNamara 1991) can be regarded simply as an enhanced version of the common 'round robin' reports that litter teachers' in-trays. In these cases an HOY sends a slip around to staff who teach a particular child and asks for comments on their behaviour, attitude and progress. What the responses invariably confirm is that the child is generally a pain, with some individual responses indicating significant concerns and a couple of 'he's no problem with me' type comments. As a form of assessment the approach lacks rigour and is best regarded as a mechanism for building up a case against the child's right to a place at the school.

The Behaviour Survey Checklist (BSC) retains a key dimension of the round robin report; the gathering of perspectives from a range of staff. This is an important point from the behaviour support perspective. A common situation can be for the behaviour support teacher to be caught in discussions with a key player in the school, for example the SENCO or HOY. Often these staff will be highly knowledgeable about the difficulties that individual children are causing staff. They may often be the first port of call for teachers when there are incidents. They may also be the school's gatekeeper in terms of accessing behaviour support and consequently present cases that accentuate the neediness of particular pupils. It is likely that by the time the HOY/SENCO is discussing a case with the behaviour support teacher the school has already undertaken some initial 'assessment'. In some instances this might be an extensive analysis of the child's needs; in most cases the behaviour support teacher will be presented with an incident list of poor behaviour.

One of the first challenges for the behaviour support teacher endeavouring to work systemically is to introduce a contextual dimension to the assessment of a problem situation. Having access to a range of viewpoints on a child's performance can be a helpful first step and demonstrates to the referrer that the service takes seriously the school's concerns. Requesting a version of a round robin report is a relatively harmless suggestion and one that is familiar to many schools.

For some support services this is the point at which the BSC is introduced. As part of the partnership planning process, the service undertakes to copy and administer the collation of staff responses, thereby reducing the burden on the school. A copy of the checklist is distributed to every subject teacher for the child. In some instances a slightly truncated version of the checklist is given out so that staff have a two-sided A4 page to check through. The time required for a response is less than five minutes and a dozen responses will take a practised behaviour support teacher a good half an hour to 45 minutes to summarise using the summary charts. The quality and range of information generated through the process is time well spent.

The BSC provides a sophisticated profile. Unlike the conventional report system that invites ad hoc observations and comments from teachers, the checklist asks all teachers of a pupil to grade a common list of possible problem behaviours. This is the first important improvement on the conventional report process where the tendency is on detailing only what the child cannot do. In gathering responses to a common list from a group of teachers on an individual child a number of highly valuable observations can be made. An example of a completed summary pro forma is shown in Figure 2.7. These charts can enable the behaviour support teacher to make some fairly conventional findings:

- identifying which behaviours cause most problems for teachers;
- the extent to which problem behaviour is experienced across the staff group;
- the level of concern individual teachers have regarding specific behaviours.

Because teachers are responding to a common predetermined list of behaviours it is also possible for the support teacher to determine:

- which behaviours are of little or no concern, in other words where the child is most successful;
- where teachers differ in identifying 'no-problem' behaviours.

Because the BSC summarises responses per subject the behaviour support teacher can also begin to deduce:

- overlaps between high concerns of problem behaviours and subject areas;
- subject areas where little if any problem behaviour occurs.

Because the summary charts also show the level of concern per behaviour the support teacher can also start to pick out which behaviours most need to be addressed and how this links with staff perceptions. Finally, because the behaviours are clustered into verbal, non-verbal and work skills categories, it is possible to make some initial conclusions about the needs of a pupil. For example, where there is a high level of concern regarding work skill behaviours it may be worth making additional enquiries regarding specific or moderate learning needs.

The summarising of a pupil's performance using the BSC provides the behaviour support service with several routes into setting up systemic intervention.

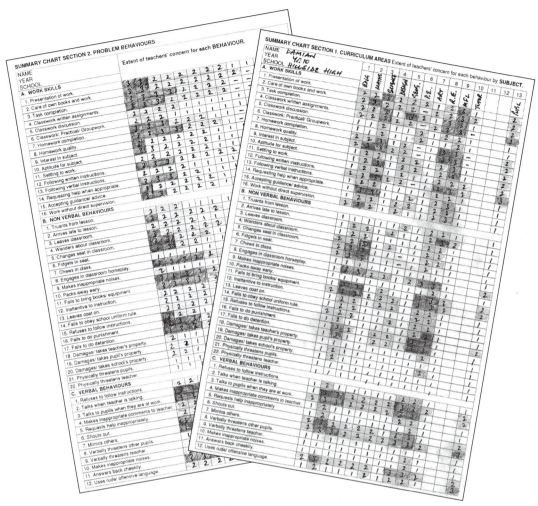

Figure 2.7 A sample completed summary pro forma

- First, although the assessment was essentially focused on a pupil, the profile generates as much information about staff perceptions.
- Second, it begins to provide some answers to that fundamental systemic question: when does the problem behaviour not occur?
- Third, it gives the behaviour support teacher direction as to which behaviours need to be addressed if negative staff perceptions about the child are to be changed.
- Fourth, the approach helps the behaviour support teacher explore beyond the case as initially presented at referral.

Using *TBB* Part 2: Assessment

The second component of the *TBB* approach that can make a significant contribution to moving behaviour support forward is the assessment material. While the BSC has a distinct secondary phase emphasis, the *Towards Better Behaviour: Part 2 Assessment* (Jolly and McNamara 1992) resource can be easily applied in both primary and secondary settings. At the centre of the material is the observation schedule which, as with the BSC, is based on behavioural theory and uses the familiar method of on- and off-task, fixed interval sampling.

Many teachers, and particularly those working in SEN departments, will have come across the approach of marking whether a child is on- or off-task at a given interval of five minutes, for example. Often this method is used where there are concerns about the limited concentration of a pupil or their repetitive low level distracting behaviour. As a single approach to recording a particular behaviour of a child it has limitations. However, the *TBB* observation schedule is designed to generate a profile of a pupil's observed behaviour within the classroom/peer group/lesson context.

Observing pupils in lessons is a common part of many assessment approaches. However, for the most part the detail can tend to focus on the performance of the target pupil and leave contextual commentary as a peripheral dimension to the exercise. This can often reflect the basis on which the observer is contracted to be in the classroom – the child is referred for support so it follows that the observer is primarily looking at the child. Where services have not declared and contracted a systemic remit it is less likely that observational reports will focus on contextual themes.

The strength of the *TBB* observation schedule is that it enables the observer to use the conventional interval sampling method to explore a rich dynamic: a pupil (or pupils) within the context of their peers, during the development of a lesson within a single classroom environment, led by a particular teacher. Unlike conventional observational approaches to behaviour, the *TBB* material can give the behaviour support specialist an abundance of valuable information within a single lesson's observation.

The observation schedules can provide the behaviour support teacher with raw data that can be transformed into extremely useful feedback to subject/class teachers. An example of a completed schedule and summary charts are shown in Figure 2.8. The approach gives the teacher a detailed picture of their class that is not delivered through performance management, appraisal or inspection processes. If managed sensitively the majority of teachers are extremely appreciative of this level of detailed observation. More standard observational approaches generate details regarding an individual child that may or may not be of immediate interest to an individual teacher. However, a more holistic, whole-class approach that includes coverage of classroom and teaching based factors invariably engages teachers in constructive discussions about the dynamic relationship between teacher, children, curriculum and environment.

In addition to the observation schedule, the *TBB* resource also includes a series of additional checklists which the observer can use when not recording the on-/off-task behaviour of pupils. These cover a wide range of factors ranging from classroom-based features and pupil and curriculum factors, through to particular types of teacher interaction. The checklists are designed so that the observer can provide evidence-based feedback with supplementary strategies for resolving factors that contribute to unwanted, off-task behaviour.

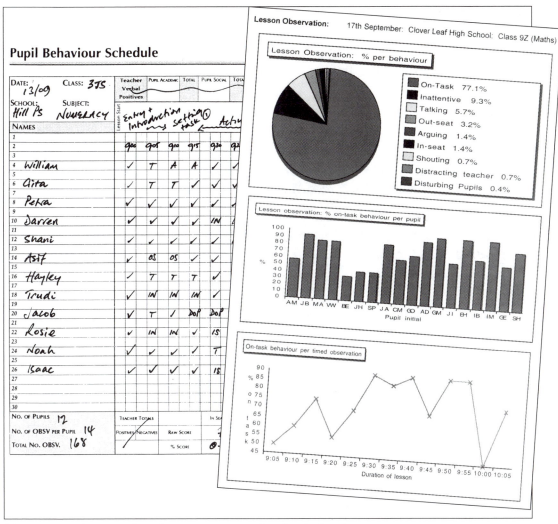

Figure 2.8 A completed summary and schedule chart

Clearly the business of class observation is beset with potential difficulty. In particular, clarifying the rationale for observation/team teaching and managing the feedback to teachers can be a highly sensitive but necessary part of the process. The following guidance is worthwhile considering when developing either observation or team teaching as part of behaviour support intervention.

Observing colleagues and team teaching: guidance notes

The task of observing colleagues at work is a peculiarly contentious aspect in the teaching profession. Observation has been closely associated with inspection and appraisal which are linked to judging performance, about which teachers often have legitimate concerns.

However, watching colleagues at work can also be one of the most effective approaches to not only developing individual practice, but also to improving the collective professional competence of the staff team. This does not simply mean that one group of teachers learn skills from another, but that the awareness of whole-school community experiences increases across all staff.

In planning team teaching and observation it is important to establish a series of core understandings:

- that the activity is not part of a formal appraisal/inspection/competency process;
- that both participants anticipate expanding respective insights into professional practice;
- that any written records of the activity are jointly owned and that there is an agreement as to which records are shared with other parties.

In negotiating arrangements for either observation or team teaching the partnership planning principles detailed earlier in this chapter should be considered. For the particular purpose of observation or team teaching the following planning questions might be addressed. The respective contracting principles are indicated in parentheses.

- When will the activity take place, in which classroom, what teaching group will be observed (procedural)?
- Is the observer sufficiently briefed in terms of the context of the lesson, for example subject knowledge, lesson plan, needs of the group, and is the observed class teacher aware of the observation method being used (professional)?
- Are both parties clear as to why the observation/team teaching is taking place? How will each party know that the observation has been successful (purpose)?
- What will the partnership look like in action? Define specifically the respective roles – for observation who will tell the pupils about the observer, how will this be done, where there is team teaching who will lead on praising/sanctioning youngsters, directing the work of non-teaching staff, introducing a theme etc. (process)?
- How might the observation fail? What happens if target pupils are absent? What if the lesson significantly deteriorates? Or the observer arrives late? Or the observer is unfamiliar with names and needs of pupils? How will both parties ensure that there will be time for feedback – this is the most common problem in carrying out effective observation (psychological)?
- How do the parties anticipate using the observation/team teaching experience? How do they hope it will inform further change in practice? How will the information shape future support (*physis*)?

With specific regard to observation, the following may also be helpful: Argyris (in Watkins and Wagner 2000) offers a handful of valuable pointers for team teachers and observers which can be summarised as follows:

- Be clear beforehand about any evaluative dimension of the observation.
- The support teacher should ask colleagues if there are any aspects they would want feedback on and to be explicit about their intended focus.
- Afterwards, when asking questions, explain the rationale for asking a question.

- Do not make judgements without clarifying their basis and having evidence drawn from the observed lesson.
- Avoid using the discussion as a control or influence interaction.

Implementing *TBB* through delivering behaviour support

The application of the *TBB* approach is varied and a number of services have used a combination of approaches, the most common of which are listed below.

- In some instances the Behaviour Survey Checklist is used right at the beginning of any work relating to an individual pupil. Before any direct support plan is drafted the behaviour support service takes on the task of administering the distribution and collation of teacher responses and generates a pupil profile. Only at this stage will the behaviour support teacher consider what course of action to take. In some cases it might be more appropriate to work with subject staff if the concerns about behaviour are solely rooted in particular curriculum areas.
- The Behaviour Survey Checklist can also be used by behaviour support staff for carrying out tracking of an individual pupil or a class across a school day. This can be an especially useful starting point for a project focused on a year group or for auditing whole-school policy.
- A number of behaviour support teams use the observation schedule as an initial starting point working on the assumption that seeing a child or group in a normal class context is a useful first step in assessment. Where a pupil's off-task behaviour is pronounced it might then be suggested that the survey checklist is used.
- On the other hand, some services have used a series of checklist summaries to best determine which lessons to then observe, using the observation schedule.
- When using the observation schedule behaviour support teachers have found that if a recording of teachers' verbal interaction is to be made this needs to be explicitly contracted with the teacher prior to the observation. It is best to work on the assumption that this aspect of the schedule is not used unless expressly requested.
- In using the checklist some services have found it useful to ask the young person to complete a pro forma. This can be especially valuable in identifying correlation and difference between the perceptions of staff and pupil about problem behaviour.

One of the most significant and understated advantages of the *TBB* approach lies in its behavioural roots. Both the observation schedule and the BSC provide extremely useful baseline information in a quantitative format. This has enormous implications for strengthening the evaluation of behaviour support input and this theme is discussed more fully in Chapter 4: Monitoring and evaluation.

As with any approach, there are some limitations to the *Towards Better Behaviour* model and these in part lie with its behavioural roots. For instance:

- Colleagues have rightly pointed to the difficulties in relying on an observation schedule that records only observable behaviour. The observation schedule involves using a series of codes for off-task behaviour – for example, T= talking, A=arguing, IN=inattentiveness etc. Care needs to be taken when using the codes so that, for example, task-related discussion is recorded differently from non-task talking, or that the pupil who appears to be simply gazing out of the window daydreaming is not in fact calculating a complex mental maths sum. Decisions will need to be made by the observer and the key watchwords are 'consistency' and 'communication'. Whatever decision is made in one instance needs to be consistent with how the next incident is recorded and the difficulties in recording need to be shared with the teacher in the feedback.
- An obvious limitation in using the observation schedule is that pupil behaviour can change dramatically from lesson to lesson (it is also worth noting that teacher behaviour tends to change across a week, as do the classroom environments that adults and children work in!). More specifically the weakness of fixed interval recording is that it fails to capture the detail of behaviour occurring outside of the fixed point of recording. Consequently a child might happen to be on-task at the point of recording but then creating mayhem between intervals.

There are some steps that behaviour support staff can take to minimise these difficulties. First, it is recommended that the behaviour support teacher does not rely on a single observation when assessing need and potential interventions. In most cases it will be necessary to carry out observations at least at differing times of the day and week and ideally across a range of curriculum areas/subject staff and peer groups where appropriate. Second, in the case of the limitations of the fixed interval method, a shorter period between recordings might be used and making additional narrative notes about behaviour incidents is usually possible with relatively little pressure on the observer's time and attention.

Another issue that is raised is that the Behaviour Survey Checklist relies on the subjective perceptions of individual staff and does not offer an objective view of a pupil's profile. Staff perceptions can change, especially where they are being required to complete the pro forma on the basis of a first reaction to each item. If they have just taught the child when they complete the form it is possible that the response would be different than if they had not worked with them for a week. While this creates difficulties for those adopting a more purist behavioural perspective, the emphasis on staff perceptions – whether stable or fluctuating – is a dividend from a systemic perspective. If the behaviour support teacher is seeking to understand and intervene systemically then the changing perceptions of staff are the essence of the work.

All in all the *TBB* model provides the behaviour support team with a range of resources that can be very powerful in terms of establishing a systemic service for schools. The effectiveness of the material is entirely dependent on the partnership planning which precedes their use. The observation schedule will not succeed as an entry point for staff development work or group work unless the support teacher contracted to do so. The potential for developing whole-school approaches through the BSC profiling is redundant if the service does not have a robust contracting method. While the material has some technical limitations it remains arguably the most useful identification and assessment approach that services can use for developing systemic support.

Schools as organisations: making contact, engaging with school culture and initiating change

Many colleagues involved in delivering behaviour support will be aware of the numerous audit tools now available for assessing the effectiveness of whole school approaches. The increased emphasis on whole-school policy development culminated in the government's *Social Inclusion: Pupil Support* guidance (DfEE 1999) with the requirement that all schools have a behaviour policy. Consequently many schools have been occupied with the process of surveying the views and ideas of staff, parents and, in the best cases, pupils too. Similarly, for those schools involved in the national Healthy Schools programme, parental and pupil surveys are an integral part of the preparatory stage.

From a behaviour support perspective this auditing activity provides an important opportunity to explore the school's internal relationships and identify the most appropriate points of engagement. Implicit in the process is an exploration of the school ethos. Messages about the values, intentions and aspirations of the school community can be identified which can give clues about how best to work with the school effectively. A subtle distinction to make here is between the *type* of behaviour support intervention and the more complex question of *how* support is developed with the school.

Case study: Understanding the audience

Let us take an example in more detail: the behaviour support teacher has been involved in supporting the audit of a school's approach to behaviour. The exercise identifies the common difficulty around consistency among teachers in using praise and sanctions. A legitimate area for development might be to use some general behavioural material, for example, the rules-praise-ignore (RPI) technique with groups of staff. Many support teachers are familiar with the material and it can make a significant impact on improving general behaviour in the classroom.

However, the task of actually making the intervention happen can become entangled in issues that prevent the work being successful or taking place at all. In some schools the work fails because staff simply do not attend the training sessions, in others, objections are raised by teachers about the mechanistic nature of the RPI approach. In some instances staff argue that consistency in technique suppresses an individual approach, while in another, concerns are raised about how the needs of individual children

---

might be accommodated through using a common approach. Of course, there will also be those schools where colleagues are highly appreciative of a systematic and structured approach through which teachers can most effectively manage children's behaviour!

From the perspective of the behaviour support teacher, the *process* of supporting teachers can be the key factor for success. Getting the process right is arguably the biggest challenge – even greater than deciding *what* to do with colleagues. In establishing effective work with schools it is necessary for the behaviour support service to have an understanding of how school culture determines the rules for engagement. Understanding school culture will determine whether or not the support teacher makes effective contact with the school and brings about change.

Doors to success and failure

To help understand how behaviour support teams might effectively work within a school culture it is worthwhile introducing a concept drawn from the work of Paul Ware who used the ideas in working with clients in a therapeutic relationship (see Ware 1983). The concept has been adapted in relation to business organisations by Critchley and Casey (1989) and I offer a further adaption here in relation to working with schools. The model offers a really helpful way of unpicking how it is that our approaches to support schools can sometimes work and in other instances do not even get off the ground. The model works on the assumption that the behaviour and attitude of the behaviour support teacher is critically important in determining success – the behaviour team are as inextricably linked into the dynamic of any intervention as mainstream teachers and children.

It is important at the outset to understand the basis of the rules of engagement, as reflected in Ware's therapeutic work. In broad terms, communication between people takes the form of one of three channels which are thinking, feeling and doing. At the heart of the model are three figurative doors which relate to corresponding types of connection with a client or, in the work of a behaviour support teacher, a school system. They are referred to as:

- The initial contact door: this relates to the type of communication that best establishes initial acceptance and trust within a school.
- The door for change: this relates to the type of communication that is the most appropriate focus for introducing change to a particular school.
- The trap door: this relates to styles of communication that will be least effective for a particular school.

Dependent on the culture of the organisation, each door can be 'opened' through adopting a particular channel of communication. Before exploring this concept any further, it is important to consider the range of school culture that services find themselves working with and a possible typology is provided in Figure 2.9. The range of types is not offered as a definitive or prescriptive listing but provides a helpful starting point for using the three doors of engagement model. Experience indicates that no one school will fall neatly within a single typology. As discussed earlier, schools cannot be understood as monolithic – they hold a range of contending groups and competing agendas. Nevertheless, particular schools do have a dominant culture underpinned by values that are more highly prized and regarded than others and this does not deny the existence of subculture(s) within a school. School culture is a concept that is frequently referred to but can also remain elusive. (For further consideration of how school culture might be assessed and for more detailed discussion about the typology which is based on the transactional analysis ego-state model, see Barrow *et al.* 2001.)

Type of culture	General features
Directive	The school has clear structures in terms of procedures and policy and has a strong sense of hierarchy and authority. The emphasis on structure is well pronounced and demonstrated by a reliance on the use of behavioural techniques in the classroom and a tight focus on raising academic achievement. School traditions are highly valued and staffroom etiquette reflects the importance of status and power. Prevailing pedagogy is based on traditional values of teacher as imparting knowledge to inexperienced pupils. Staff relations tend to be grounded in the hierarchical structure with the head teacher being 'protected' by an inner sanctum of senior staff. The school has a keen sense of its history and achievement. The school may also have a strong sense of protecting staff and pupils through a paternalistic pastoral support system. HOYs or Head of House staff have a particular importance in secondary schools of this type. In a primary school the SENCO or Deputy might be strongly associated with maintaining a particularly nurturing role on behalf of the organisation. The emphasis on structure can provide a sense of security for staff and pupils, particularly during times of difficulty. In relation to managing behaviour, teachers will be clear what strategies are available for responding to difficult behaviour and pupils will be well aware of what constitutes unacceptable performance. However, some staff and pupils might also feel over-controlled and the implicit power-relationship in the school might alienate particular groups of pupils and less senior members of staff, including support staff. While the nurturing aspect of the school adds to the sense of security for staff and pupils, it can also be regarded as intrusive by some groups and can limit the potential for individual autonomy. In the Directive school culture, the priority is on achievement. The dominant channel of communication is through doing.

Figure 2.9 Typology of school culture

Type of culture	General features
	From a behaviour support perspective, *under stress* these schools tend to: • emphasise that they have already used a range of strategies (which did not work); • emphasise their history of experience in working with 'difficult pupils'; • discuss pupils as having problems, poor background, complicated difficulties and/or a notion of 'bad' kids; • hold the view that if they cannot cope with a situation, then no one else can; • generally resist the involvement of external agencies (because the school sees itself as managing very effectively without them).
Informative	The school has a strong business organisation ethos. The emphasis is on clarity about staff roles and responsibilities, as opposed to hierarchy and power. Decision making is firmly based on evidence and the emphasis on data collation and analysis is pronounced. Approaches to managing behaviour tend towards cognitive, problem-solving approaches; circle time is used for discussion and negotiation, pastoral care focuses on structured counselling aimed at pupils being challenged to think about their behaviour. Staff relationships are maintained at a highly professional level with an emphasis on using formal meetings and structured consultation to inform planning and resolve difficulties. The school is run efficiently and there is a sense of precision and accuracy in how staff assess situations. Staff and pupils are well organised and have a clear sense of purpose. There will be frequent reference to developmental plans, milestones and targets – the direction of the school will have been well thought through and clearly presented. The businesslike approach gives staff and pupils a clear sense of their role and expectations, which can provide security. The emphasis on analysis and problem-solving techniques means that the school is often very successful in meeting developmental goals. Difficulties, including crises regarding behaviour, are generally well managed. However, the focus on detailed planning can mean that some staff and pupils can be constrained by what feels like inflexible and predetermined structure. The potential for individual growth and expression is compromised by the more general emphasis on efficient organisational development.

Figure 2.9 continued

Type of culture	General features
	In an Informative school culture the priority is on structure. The dominant channel of communication is through thinking. From a behaviour support perspective, *under stress* these schools tend to: • be over-detailed about the nature of a child's difficulty with supporting assessment evidence; • have a rigid understanding of what the child needs; • emphasise that individual 'pupils with problems' find it difficult to 'fit in' to the school system – their needs are beyond that which the school can accommodate given their resources and expectations; • focus more on the level of potential support and how it will integrate within existing school routines, as opposed to outcomes; • be very clear about what the support should involve and achieve and be resistant to seeing things differently; • be generally receptive to support providing it fits within existing plans or meets identified needs.
Demonstrative	The school enjoys a non-conformism. The culture of the school is earmarked by an uneven and oscillating combination of individualism and rebelliousness. Staff have considerable latitude in how they run their lessons, including the management of behaviour. There is an important emphasis on developing creativity and responding to the feelings of staff and pupils. The school might be regarded locally as eccentric or maverick and this can sometimes be linked with remarkable achievement or exasperation at its failure to achieve. The ethos of the school is very much influenced by emotional phases so that staff can reflect a tremendous sense of fun and free-spiritedness which can then shift to a position of exhaustion which in turn moves into a terrific period of industrious activity. The head teacher has enthusiastic bouts on particular themes and encourages staff and pupils to do the same. Pupils' achievements are highly valued, both academic and extra-curricular. Staff management of behaviour can centre on using circle time to explore feelings and attitudes; pupils are encouraged to talk about problems, possibly through peer counselling or adult mentoring. The school can be extremely exciting to be part of, especially when a new initiative is being explored. The use of humour is prevalent and initiative is encouraged and promoted. The sense of the school as being a family is an important element in these schools and consequently can provide security for both staff

Figure 2.9 continued

Type of culture	General features
	and pupils. However, in terms of planned, structured development these schools can be exceptionally difficult to work with. Some staff and pupils will feel uncomfortable with the level of familiarity and emphasis on feelings.

The priority in the Demonstrative school culture is person-orientated outcomes. The dominant channel of communication is feelings.

From a behaviour support perspective, *under stress* these schools tend to:

• be seductive – they can be good fun to work in, extremely welcoming and offer plenty of distraction from the task of the support teacher;
• resist detailed planning and negotiation – the pressure is on to 'come in and get going';
• emphasise what needs to be done and not consider anticipated outcome;
• be disorganised and consequently there is a potential for missed appointments, misunderstanding and conflict;
• express disappointment that individual 'poor children' cannot remain with the school;
• be emotionally temperamental – on one visit the behaviour support teacher is regarded as befriender sharing in the enthusiasm to deliver on a new project, while on the next visit he or she is to be blamed for the deterioration in behaviour! |

Figure 2.9 continued

Having identified the dominant ideology of a school it is possible to make some general comments about how the behaviour support service might best connect with the school, either to build trust and credibility, bring about change or avoid failure. A matrix for how these types of dialogue differ across the types of culture are presented in Figure 2.10.

So if we return to our example above where the BST introduces the RPI approach we can begin to understand why the idea may have faltered and failed.

• In some schools (Demonstrative) the work staff simply did not attend the training sessions (the support teacher fell through the trap door).
• In others (Informative), objections are raised by teachers about the mechanistic nature of the RPI approach (it lacks cognition – the support teacher has not spent sufficient time at the initial contact door).
• In some instances (Demonstrative), staff argue that consistency in technique suppresses an individual approach (the emphasis on structure might become acknowledged, but it is at the door for change – initial contact has not been secured by the support team).

School culture type	Door for initial contact	Door for change	Trap door
Directive	It is important for the behaviour support teacher (BST) to acknowledge the existing experience and success that the school has in the identified area for support. The BST will need to work at their most tactful and be accepting of the sense of outrage that this type of school can express, even if the BST regards it as an over reaction or misplaced. The hostility that this type of school can generate needs to be taken seriously and the BST should avoid an immediate challenge if they are to be trusted by the school.

Building up a detailed account of what strategies have already been tried is important in demonstrating that the BST acknowledges the experience of the school and can also give clues for next steps.

The channel for initial communication is *doing*. | The language of thinking and encouraging a problem-solving approach tends to be most effective for the BST in supporting change in this type of culture. If this strategy is deployed before adequate contact has been achieved staff will not feel that their concerns have been acknowledged or accepted and consequently tend to rebuff BST suggestions.

The BST might use a range of phrases including: 'What do you think might happen if?' 'How do you think that things might change if?' 'What do you think should happen?'

The channel for change communication is *thinking*. | Creativity, humour, perceived lack of organisation and respect for school hierarchy and protocols are the most efficient ways of destroying any chance of effective work within this school culture. In these circumstances behaviour support is likely to be regarded at best as eccentric and at worst unprofessional.

Similarly focusing on the emotional needs of a child – or member of staff – is unlikely to be a helpful starting point. It is worth keeping at the forefront of thinking that the school presents as affronted by the identified difficulty (it may be that at a psychological level the school is threatened by the behaviour, and directly addressing this emotional need is a definite trap door!).

During times of pressure the school will fall back on core values and expectations – any notion of unstructured, free-spirited approaches will lack credibility and be doomed from the start.

Another approach worth avoiding is directly challenging the values of the |

Figure 2.10 The three doors of engagement

School culture type	Door for initial contact	Door for change	Trap door
			school – the identity, stability and survival of the culture is highly dependent on the inviolability of its traditions and beliefs. The channel for trap door communication is *feeling*.
Informative	The school is more likely to be confident with the BST if due consideration and regard are given to its capacity to have assessed and identified possible interventions. The key feature to remember in building trust within this culture is the respect for analysis and thinking. The BST will need to evidence-base its proposals and should emphasise monitoring and evaluation – especially the quantitative dimension. Engaging colleagues in partnership planning will be relatively straightforward and it will be important to explicitly locate BST intervention within related school plans. Using problem-solving language with references to thinking will be helpful in initial discussions. While the school will be tolerant of an informal approach, including humour, the BST should not	One of the most helpful ways to encourage a development of this type of culture can be to encourage creativity and innovation. Providing that proposals are rooted in a sound rationale the school can be committed to projects that extend its knowledge and experience base. Promoting key aspects of intervention can lead the school to take on more challenging work. These aspects include: • monitoring and evaluation (measuring progress informs thinking); • dissemination (up-skilling colleagues is part of being a learning organisation); • links to research and theory (this legitimises the activity and gives it a rationale and structure).	The BST needs to avoid being regarded as either too controlling or too informal. The culture resists interference from colleagues who rely on status without regard for evidence-based argument. Similarly, the BST who is less concerned with planning and structuring their work will find difficulties in engaging with the school. While using humour is acceptable, it comes second place to a seriousness about the task in hand. Focusing on the importance of feelings can have a limited effect as this can be regarded as an unhelpful distraction from effective problem solving. Another pitfall can be for the BST to nurture colleagues. This will be regarded as quite inappropriate in this

Figure 2.10 continued

School culture type	Door for initial contact	Door for change	Trap door
	underestimate the importance of being regarded as efficient and businesslike. The channel for initial communication is *thinking*.	The school is unlikely to be too adventurous until it has built trust in the ability of the BST to demonstrate that they have an efficient working practice, underpinned by sound theory and analysis. The channel of communication for change is *feeling*.	type of organisation. Colleagues will not want tea and sympathy – they will be seeking a clear plan to resolve difficulty efficiently delivered. The channel for trap door communication is *doing*.
Demonstrative	The style of initial contact communication is centred around feelings and doing. For the BST this means responding enthusiastically to proposed ideas, using humour and most important, acknowledging the distinct character of the school. If colleagues have any sense of tradition it will be as either a bunch of rebels or mavericks where there is a 'brilliant' staff atmosphere. This will have been carefully maintained over the years and the BST will do well to nurture it. Creative proposals for support will often appeal and the school may enjoy being part of a pilot for a new project. In many of these schools the importance of emotional growth and the links with	The door for change in this culture is to introduce thinking and structure. Often the emphasis on intuitive responses to situations can leave children and staff vulnerable where there is little underpinning structure. Similarly, with a relatively limited emphasis on thinking, situations can arise due to lack of planning and/or analysis. Through a genuine sense of care for staff and pupils it is possible to introduce colleagues to important change through asking some of the thinking/problem-solving questions featured in the Directive section above. The BST needs to carefully consider when to shift from initial contact to the	It is crucial for the BST to avoid trying to control and over-structure their work in this type of culture. This is the type of school where local inspectors are given short shrift and where the more formal aspects of the education system – league tables, National Curriculum requirements, target setting etc. – are most loudly derided. Consequently it is important that the BST does not initiate contact with an overly formal planning process and bombard colleagues with details of protocols – these staff just want to get started. Although working in this type of school can be very enjoyable there are some real frustrations in terms of planning, monitoring and evaluation. The BST

Figure 2.10 continued

School culture type	Door for initial contact	Door for change	Trap door
	learning – with a heavy emphasis on self-esteem – should be appreciated and acknowledged by the BST. Giving time to listen to staff express their feelings about a situation will be important and having time to hear about the feelings and difficulties of pupils will be equally valued in this culture. The important factors in determining the credibility of the BST will not hang on their organisational skill or regard for hierarchy, but on whether they really understand what it feels like to work in the organisation. The channel for initial communication is most likely to be *feeling* although this can be substituted for *doing* in some cases.	change dialogue. Mis-timing the move can leave colleagues believing that their feelings have been ignored and that the BST lacks sensitivity. In most cases the channel for change will be *thinking* although *feeling* will be the likely alternative.	needs to resist the temptation of taking over and controlling the intervention. Aside from limiting the sustainability of the intervention, other consequences can be that the BST is left to do the work while the others become interested in new and more exciting tasks, or the BST is blamed for any project failure! In most cases the channel of trap door communication will be *doing* although in these schools *thinking* will be the likely alternative.

Figure 2.10 continued

- While in another (Demonstrative, and possibly Informative) concerns about how the needs of individual children might be accommodated through using a common approach are raised. (The staff in the Informative culture are figuring out the practical implications of some youngsters not being adequately accommodated within the technique. Once again, the support teacher will need to build up more credibility before moving on to the door for change. Those in the Demonstrative culture are anxious that the support team is abandoning the needs of an important minority who are specially vulnerable, or ignoring the strong feelings that staff have about a particular group of pupils. In this case the support teacher may be perilously close to a trap door scenario!)
- Of course, there will also be those schools (Directive) where colleagues are highly appreciative of a systematic and structured approach through which teachers can most effectively manage children's behaviour. (The behaviour support teacher hits the jackpot in making a step change in introducing some structuring to the work of teachers.)

These ideas about how behaviour support teams engage with schools are at the earliest stages of development. Early use of the material indicates that it has much to commend its use in helping us reflect on why we are successful in some schools and how we become stuck in others. Given the shift towards behaviour support being based from within individual schools, it is arguably even more critical that support teams find effective routes in understanding work with organisational culture.

3 Delivering effective behaviour support

Having explored approaches to negotiating, planning and assessing intervention, this section focuses on a range of strategies used by behaviour support specialists for delivering support. While a number of pupil-focused approaches are presented, the emphasis throughout the section is on practical ways of working systemically with schools.

In the early years of behaviour support development there was a tendency for services to adopt a particular theoretical perspective and shape practice in accordance with corresponding techniques. Consequently a number of support services developing during the immediate post-Elton Report period (1989) were predominantly concerned with introducing behavioural theory and technique in supporting pupils and schools. During the early 1990s there was a rapid growth in the range and amount of regional and national interest in derivations on behaviour management, including the popular work of Wheddall and Merritt's BATPACK (and the longstanding prevalence of Lee Canter's Assertive Discipline movement). The practice reflected a rising trend in the use of cognitive behavioural techniques by many educational psychology services across the country.

In the recent past a number of services have increasingly become wary of relying on a single theoretical perspective, choosing instead to draw from a more eclectic range of options. While these services have a preferred perspective they commonly use strategies from cognitive, behavioural and psychodynamic theories. In these instances services move closer to delivering a systemic model of support.

One way in which we might understand how systemic support draws from across a range of perspectives is through a tool kit analogy. Nowadays most DIY tasks involve a cross-head screwdriver. Whenever you buy a flat-pack item you can bet your bottom dollar that you will need that Phillips screwdriver. You may also be fairly sure that you will need a drill and possibly a hammer (although this seems to be a necessity for all of *my* jobs, in addition to fluent Anglo-Saxon). However, with an increasing range of flat-pack designs and associated fittings there are often specific tools needed to complete the job, some of which are actually provided in the pack.

In turning up at a school to develop support I have found that there are some 'tools' that experience shows are almost always needed to tackle whatever work arises. In my metaphorical toolbox these are solution-focused brief therapy questions. Readers may be familiar with this approach and the unique potential it offers in building up a partnership with colleagues (for additional commentary on its use in schools see Long and Fogell 1999). I am confident that within the first meeting I will have asked variations on the following:

• Tell me how you have been managing with this situation so far?
• What is it that you would ideally like to happen? What would be the impact of that change on how the pupil/teacher/group behaved?
• When does the difficulty *not* occur?
• Tell me, what do you do really well?

Mark Provis in his work on using systemic theory in behaviour support refers to the 'one down response' in which the perceived expert is giving the message 'I need your help to understand this'. Personally I have also found the 'Columbo technique' can be similarly effective, whereby the specialist adopts a 'strategic incompetence' (Provis 1992). The solution-focused approach is securely rooted in systemic theory; in its purest form there is no place for problem identification or diagnosis as these clearly distract the supporter from discovering potential resources, previous achievement and a sense of a preferred future. Another important dimension implicit in the approach, which is often worth making explicit, is that the behaviour support teacher has no pretensions to being an expert in the client's area of difficulty. Bill O'Hanlon, a well-established solution-focused practitioner, puts it like this: ' . . . We do see clients as experts in their own lives, on what is bothering them and how they want their lives to be . . . [the solution-focused practitioner] considers [themselves] as expert in the change process' (O'Hanlon and Beadle 2000).

While the history of solution-focused brief therapy lies in family therapy and social work applications, it is fast becoming a credible and popular technique for use in educational settings. Several services have used the approach in working directly with children (see Stringer and Mall 1999) and others have incorporated the techniques in providing supervision for support team members and mainstream colleagues. While the partnership planning approach is primarily drawn from a transactional analysis concept, several key elements of the negotiation (and pre-negotiation) phase are peppered with solution-focused-type questions. This systemic approach is the metaphorical equivalent of my cross-head screwdriver.

The solution-focused questions are always extremely useful for getting started on a case, in the same way that there are always bits of the flat pack that can be readily assembled just with the screwdriver. On an extremely occasional basis a presenting difficulty might be entirely resolved through only using the one approach – the process of partnership planning, for example, might help school staff more precisely identify what it is they can do without support in order to resolve a situation. Regardless of whether the approach resolves a difficulty, the responses to the questions generate important information which can be used for informing planning for intervention.

In most cases I find myself needing to use other tools which have become familiar. I can expect to use concepts taken from psychological theory, specifically transactional analysis, which can illuminate the potential and actual emotional dynamic. I also frequently find myself helping colleagues recall their background knowledge and experience of using behavioural techniques, with a particular emphasis on the consistent use of reinforcement. This collection of approaches, each being pulled from different theoretical bases, forms a basic tool kit.

However, the ultimate task for the systemic behaviour specialist is to ensure that the tool kit is not regarded as a box of magic tricks – the best quality practice involves the support teacher handing over the tool kit complete with theory and technique. This is an important point which deserves reiteration:

> ...effective management of behaviour may really require ways of improving teachers' understanding of behaviour theory rather than just off-the-shelf techniques for managing classroom incidents. (Kinder *et al.* 1999)

If behaviour support does not involve 'handing over the goods' then its impact will by implication be limited.

To complete the tool kit metaphor, I referred to the specialised widget that is used for particular fixings and that is included in the flat pack. Without this the kit cannot be completed, regardless of whether you remembered to bring your screwdriver and hammer. I am struck by how often, in discussions with school staff, a key internal element is identified that is crucial to the success of an intervention. It might be the tight working practice of the HOY team, the capacity of the school to provide sufficient non-contact time for a key member of staff, or the positive impact of an adult or peer on the behaviour of a pupil. Each of these is unique to the school's situation and is pivotal to the success of the work.

Having offered a personal introduction to this section the focus now shifts to considering particular strategies and resources that contribute to delivering systemic behaviour support. Given the emphasis throughout this book on staff and school development it makes sense to begin with a few ideas that have proven successful in developing colleagues' confidence and ability in working with problem behaviour.

Ideas for working with governors and school managers

In working with the powerful players in a school the key message for the behaviour support teacher is to keep the eye on the big picture. Governors should not be spending time on the minutiae of the conduct code and reward and sanctioning arrangements. The aim of the support teacher should be to encourage governors and leadership teams to reflect on issues around core values, school purpose and the quality of relationships. The only procedural concerns that this group could well spend time on will be on monitoring and analysing *school* behaviour. The following is a summary of a governor training programme and includes a series of questions that are extremely effective in encouraging constructive debate at an appropriately strategic level.

From little acorns: the role of governors in developing behaviour policy

Being a school governor is often a difficult role, and especially with regard to the task of establishing behaviour policy. The potential for governors to become involved in the detail of classroom management or perhaps to be sidelined in discussions about behaviour is very real. Governors can often believe that the business of dealing with behaviour in school is the sole territory of the experts – that they should not meddle with teachers' practice. On the other hand there are governors who become frustrated at being regarded as 'rubber stampers'; a group that simply endorses predetermined decisions on policy direction and exclusion matters. It is a difficult dilemma – how might the governing body both challenge and support their school?

A possible framework for resolving some of the difficulties around the task of behaviour policy is to consider the image of an oak tree. Readers will be familiar with the shape of a traditional oak – a large, full crown of foliage and a sturdy thick trunk, with an indication at ground level of a substantial root system running deep into the earth. Often when we start to think about developing policy on behaviour our attention is first drawn to the obvious themes:

- What should teachers do when children misbehave?
- How might we reward good behaviour?
- What rules should we have in the classroom or playground?

It is these aspects of whole-school approach that are the most visible – like the crown on the oak – they cover aspects of practice that appear to be immediately important. The discussions around what are essentially techniques can then tend to develop into heated debates about the issue of consistency. Teachers and school managers focus on how best to ensure greater consistency in *managing* behaviour.

The discussion around consistency is important, but it is questionable as to whether the focus should initially be on rules, rewards and sanctions. Similarly, schools can spend a great deal of time in considering the procedures for managing (mis)behaviour:

- Who should be responsible for dealing with low-level disruption, pupils sent out of class, highly disruptive incidents?
- How might referral systems integrate with the school's SEN, curriculum and pastoral arrangements?
- What is the role of the class teacher/tutor regarding the management of behaviour?

Once again, there is an understandable need to clarify these issues. The system that supports staff in using techniques is less apparent, but crucial for maintaining a whole-school approach, just as the oak's trunk underpins the crown. However, this area may also not be the most helpful starting point for governors becoming involved in developing policy.

In developing or reviewing school behaviour policy the starting point must be a discussion around core themes:

- What are the *values* that lie at the centre of our being a school community?
- What *principles* and *aims* are we committed to as a school?
- What kind of *relationships* do we want to build within our school community?

These are the roots of behaviour policy development. They may not be the most obvious starting points but they are by far the most critical in shaping what happens around the school.

If schools are keen to develop teacher consistency then the focus at the outset should be on encouraging a coherent understanding among staff of what they most value, what are their aims, for the children and themselves, and what kind of relationships they are seeking to promote. It will be far more profitable to spend a professional development day on these tasks than leap-frogging into discussions about what to do when children shout out or bully others or flout uniform rules.

Discussion around the roots of policy development should be the focus for governor involvement. Process and technique are invariably about managing behaviour at school. Hopefully this is not simply focused on pupils but addresses adult behaviour too. In general terms these aspects can remain the domain of the practitioners and managers. Establishing clarity regarding values, aims and relationships is more centred on setting a quality standard for the school. It is inextricably linked to the wider development and maintenance of school ethos and purpose and this is prime territory for governors.

If the school is clear at the outset about its policy roots, then discussions around process and technique will be more effective and arguably straightforward. Support from governors at this early stage will have dividends in the latter part of the process. Let us return to the image of the tree and introduce the concept of sap rising from the base, through the trunk and into the highly visible crown. We can perhaps see how the input of governors in helping to set the tone of approach can feed into the established techniques and processes of classroom practice.

In contributing to the policy development process governors can generate helpful debate through asking the types of questions that prompt thinking on values, aims and relationships:

- Who might we involve in the process?
  - Staff, parents, other agencies, community groups, children?
- How might we involve them?
  - Working group, consultation exercise, focus group, school council?
- How do we know what we know about *school* behaviour – as opposed to individual children's behaviour?
- What understanding of behaviour do we have in our school?
  - Can individuals be taught to behave?
  - Are individuals able to reflect on their behaviour and think about doing things differently?
  - Is behaviour essentially motivated by how individuals feel?
  - Is behaviour understood only by looking at the context in which it takes place?

• If our school is developing new, experimental work focused on improving behaviour, how might the wider school community learn and adapt as a result of the experience?

These lines of enquiry may appear a long way from the more conventional discussions we may have had about behaviour. However, from a governor perspective they must be the priorities. Resisting the urge to be drawn into the process and technique debates is difficult but necessary. In the hurly-burly of day-to-day school life, teachers and school managers can understandably become preoccupied with the 'what to do when Johnny disrupts' type of questions. The role of governors should be legitimately focused on the longer term and safeguard the aspirations for the school – for both staff and children.

Ideas for training whole-school staff and smaller groups of staff

One of the first temptations worth resisting is working on the basis that giving colleagues 'top tips for the classroom' is somehow good enough behaviour support input. It is not, because for every success a teacher has in using a top tip, there will be times when a technique does not work. Responsible behaviour support involves exposing the theoretical principles that underpin a strategy. When strategies fail in the classroom the tendency can be for teachers to fall into a precarious 'either/or' trap; either the pupil is 'beyond the pale' or they, the teacher, must be inadequate. Such a position is untenable and can be deeply damaging for both teachers and children:

> It is common for educators having difficulty [with behaviour] to understand the situation as one in which either there is something wrong with the other person or they are incompetent. Such … perspectives make cooperation difficult, encourage negative rather than positive descriptions of the problem and stifle creativity.   (Molnar and Lindquist 1989)

The work of the behaviour support teacher can be instructive for teachers at two levels. First, by generating insights about behaviour theory we can encourage teachers to shift from an 'either/or' scenario towards being more critical of a particular theoretical perspective. In other words the teacher no longer damns a pupil, or takes on guilt and feelings of inadequacy, but recognises a technique as limited by its theoretical background. The intention is for the support teacher to take some of the heat out of the immediate situation through shifting feelings of blame into a critique of the technique and theory.

Second, it is arguably time that the teaching profession made a significant move forward in professionalising its understanding and response to problem behaviour. Anecdotal evidence over the years demonstrates that when it comes to the area of behaviour, individual teachers have to figure it out for themselves. However, in relation to other important areas of professional work, for example literacy and numeracy, teachers have undergone a rapid and steep learning curve in terms of understanding theory and technique. The underlying convention on behaviour has tended to emphasise the cult of the personality as a teacher's best form of defence. The old adage of not smiling before Christmas continues to be passed down to the next generation of new teachers, and stories of 'personality clashes' between staff and children abound. Whether or not the 'no Christmas, no smile' approach works, what is unhelpful is the lack of any critical appreciation of why it might be an effective strategy and why it may not work for some teachers. Similarly, pointing out that there is a 'clash of personalities' hardly helps a teacher who needs to face the pupil the following day.

Louise Porter in her innovative work, *Behaviour in Schools* (2000), argues a convincing case for teachers taking back responsibility for responding to behaviour based on a critical understanding of current behaviour theory. She reiterates the point that technique without theory results in unsustainable practice – that 'getting on with it' can involve doing the same unsuccessful thing over and over – and instead proposes a more proactive approach:

> Once you are familiar with [behaviour theories] you can build a coherent set of ideas that helps you describe, explain and predict student behaviour and how you can respond to it. In short, you will have generated your own 'theory'. Nothing could be more relevant, useful and empowering than that.
> (Porter 2000)

The effective behaviour support teacher promotes discussion and critical appreciation of behaviour theory while also providing related techniques. There is a tactical advantage to this approach in that it allows the support teacher to pre-empt teachers' reservations about particular approaches – by presenting the limitations of techniques the support teacher avoids any hints about magic answers and demonstrates a pragmatism about the reality of the classroom. For most teachers, for most of the time, they will already be using successful strategies; the support teacher can put these within a critical framework that brings greater insight and meaning to the role of the class teacher. In summary, the main task of the support service in training activities is not about dishing out techniques, but to contribute to professionalising the work of teachers by increasing their capacity for critical appreciation of what they find themselves doing in the classroom.

Breathing life into theory: training ideas

Talking to class teachers about behaviour theory can swiftly bring about a loss of interest and scepticism. Colleagues are driven by a need to know – and be told – what to do next time kids start kicking off in lessons. Opening staff development with dry theoretical presentation is a killer. Likewise beginning with a narrative about the contemporary legislative context can also guarantee the behaviour support teacher a 15-round bout with a disgruntled staff team. The emphasis must be on working very efficiently to demonstrate what theory looks like in real terms. A few examples that I have found particularly engaging for groups are presented below.

Behavioural theory and particularly the concept of reinforcement through the technique of rule-related praise can be easily demonstrated simply through the marshalling of the group throughout the day. For example, 'Well done, this group, for getting back so swiftly from break, that was exactly what we agreed to do,' or 'thank you, this group, for listening up and being ready so that I can move on with the training'. Both of these generate humour as colleagues immediately see the rule-related technique in use but also acknowledge the swift impact it can make in drawing attention to preferred behaviour.

More specifically, the observational behavioural techniques can also be good fun to use with staff groups. Recording on-task and off-task behaviour of a number of staff can be accompanied with simultaneous commentary on the technique so that a brief summary of the observed behaviour of staff is generated to demonstrate just how much information – and hard data – can be generated through systematic observation.

Another related approach is to introduce a systemic spin to the Antecedent-Behaviour-Consequence (ABC) approach to analysing episodes of behaviour. Having considered the familiar three-stage reflective process, asking what the pupil might have been *communicating* through the episode is a valuable fourth stage that encourages colleagues to recognise that all behaviour is a means of communication.

The most effective approach I have found for demonstrating the value of **cognition** when problem solving is to guide colleagues, in pairs or threes, through a solution-focused process in which they are invited to reflect on a part of their work that they are unhappy with. This might be in relation to a particular pupil or group, or possibly a departmental or school-wide issue. Rob Long and Jonathan Fogell provide valuable ways using solution-focused techniques with staff in their work (see Long and Fogell 1999).

Perhaps the most enjoyable and engaging activities that I have found are those relating to **psychodynamic theory**. So often teachers and support staff imagine that these approaches exist outside of their domain, being the territory of mental health specialists. I am often keen to begin with asserting that for many children – and indeed some of the most vulnerable children – simply coming to school is therapeutic. Whether we choose to or not, adults in schools have an emotional impact on the well-being of pupils.

Often a lively piece of role play between the behaviour support teacher and a primed member of the staff team can be a good starting point from which to introduce the emotional experience of teaching and learning. An effective role play does not need a convoluted plot. A personal favourite is to start with an altercation over a pupil who refuses to remove their coat at the beginning of a lesson. The support teacher plays the part of a hostile and overbearing teacher, while a staff colleague revels in being an increasingly rebellious pupil, and the outburst is invariably an attention-grabbing way of opening the day or following lunch. Through exploring the emotional experience of conflict it is possible to introduce psychological theory and approaches, for example by using transactional analysis.

One of the concepts closely related to the psychodynamic approach is self-esteem. It is a phrase much bandied around education and one that can also be regarded by cynics as a catch-all response to excuse poor behaviour. I believe there is nothing quite like experiential learning and the following exercise has been a well-tried and proven approach to engaging perhaps the most reluctant staff groups.

Introducing Tommy and Tina Teacher

This exercise is a slightly adapted version of a typical circle time activity. All that is needed is two large pictures or a couple of teachers' faces, one of which has the pair clearly happy and another in which they are looking very miserable. The doodlers among the support team may choose to do a Rolf Harris and scribble the pictures as they work through the exercise, but this demands a very adept multi-tasking ability. The Gloucester primary behaviour support service has prepared a brilliantly finished series of faces for both children and teachers, well drawn, coloured and laminated for repeated use.

Start by introducing the picture of Tommy and Tina, two teachers who might well work in the school. They arrive happy and enthusiastic about the week's work ahead of them. As they walk across the school grounds at the start of the day something happens that just takes the edge off their smile.

At this point invite the staff group to make suggestions as to what can happen that can make them feel disappointed, sad or angry. Often there are a number of suggestions including:

• They have been put down for a cover lesson (and they only had a couple of non-contact sessions that week).
• They have been asked to cover a member of staff (who always seems to be away on Monday and Fridays).
• A parent meets them at the school door with a series of concerns and complaints about how they are teaching their child.
• They have to break up a fight/argument between pupils.

As the suggestions come, so the behaviour support teacher starts to cover the smiling version of the faces with parts of the second unhappy version which has been cut into small pieces. The narrative continues, following the experience of Tommy and Tina through their day, with the staff group offering suggestions for what might make the day go badly drawing on their own experience. Clearly there is a degree of risk in this exercise – staff can find themselves able to share their annoyance at a range of issues, including;

• resources not being available;
• rooms previously booked for a lesson are taken up for examinations;
• photocopier not working;
• no milk left for coffee at break-time;
• required to step in and run an assembly with no notice;
• reading the recent middlebrow tabloid teacher-bashing feature;
• a parent phoning in a complaint;
• a child misbehaving;

- a child being sick in the classroom;
- being taken for granted by colleagues;
- not being informed about a timetable change or a fire drill.

Occasionally a member of staff offers a classic comment:

'I have had a nightmare with a particular class and I wander in to the staffroom, exhausted and despairing. A colleague asks what's up and I tell her that I have had just had 9X for science. She turns and says, "Oh yes, I had them last year but I never had a problem with them."'

As these suggestions are offered so the BST continues to cover the original picture with the pieces forming an unhappy alternative until eventually all of the pieces have been used and the staff team are now looking at a picture of two very sad, despairing characters, at the end of their day at work. Throughout the exercises there is often a degree of humour and in some cases a great deal of laughter as staff are able to let off some steam about how difficult working at the school can be, without pointing blame at any individual or group. However, as the group realise that a more forlorn couple has replaced the once-happy face of two enthusiastic teachers, a sense of recognition sets in. At this point in the exercise a number of priceless observations can be made:

- How staff behave can impact on how other staff feel.
- A sense of despair and inadequacy can be linked as much to staffroom dynamics as classroom factors.
- Staff do not generally set out to make others feel bad, but they do not appreciate the cumulative impact of 'put downs' on individuals.
- We can identify with both the feelings of inadequacy and despair of Tommy/Tina and recognise ourselves in having contributed to their unhappiness.

It is a very powerful point at any stage in a staff training exercise, although arguably best left to a final whole-group activity. The support teacher can add that the profession has suffered as a result of poor staff self-esteem and that the ongoing nationwide issues about recruitment, retention and long-term sickness are proof positive of a profession with low morale.

No matter how squeezed the behaviour support teacher might be for time in this exercise, the group activity cannot be closed at this point. Often the sense of despair and sadness among a group is palpable; the power of the activity lies in its capacity to throw open a window on real emotions among a team, without exposing any single person to vulnerability. It also makes it clear that a staff team are 'in this together'.

The second phase of the activity is perhaps more powerful than the first. The narrative begins with the teachers – still using the sad picture – returning to work the following week. This time something happens as they cross the school grounds which brings a smile to their face. Colleagues are invited to offer suggestions about what happens at school that they find helpful and supportive. The support teacher leads the group through a fictitious day and as the suggestions are offered so the pieces of the sad face are removed, revealing again the original smiling faces of our two teachers. As groups are able to share how days can go so badly, so they are able to identify what can make for a caring working environment. Suggestions have included:

- asking how a colleague is feeling today;
- saying hello, *before* asking the favour;
- just saying hello;
- offering to make a coffee for a colleague who looks unhappy;
- offering to take on some administrative task, or do a break duty;
- giving some resources to a colleague teaching on a similar theme;
- sharing an appreciative comment from a child or parent/carer;
- seeing a child achieve a task, reach a goal and sharing that moment with colleagues.

There are often other comments particular to a school, but one suggestion comes up every time I run this exercise: 'Someone says "thank you", not for any special task – just for me doing my job.' This is generally followed immediately by agreeing nods and knowing glances. It is the opportunity for the behaviour support teacher to make a simple but highly effective challenge to the group: to give a thank you to a colleague by the end of the week. This could be an affirmative comment on any aspect of their practice; their neat room displays, their handling of a situation with a pupil, offering a supportive comment, providing assistance during a difficult situation. In some instances it is worth the behaviour support teacher pointing out that while praise from a school manager is especially welcome, this group does not have a monopoly on handing out thanks – all colleagues can contribute to recognising and appreciating the efforts and achievement of each other, regardless of status.

So, after this series of suggestions the group face the happy teachers we met at the beginning of the exercise. The support teacher can now reinforce the alternative observations made at the end of the first half of the exercise:

- that staff behaviour can impact on how well and able other staff feel;
- that a sense of well-being and optimism can be linked as much to staffroom dynamics as classroom factors;
- that staff may not appreciate the cumulative impact of a number of little supportive gestures on the self-esteem of an individual teacher.

It is always worth adding at some point in the exercise (and one for support staff to consider) that it is an activity that is very useful for using with groups of pupils, especially where there is a high level of name-calling, or suspicions of bullying or racism. The first part of the activity – using pictures of children – enables youngsters to share how a day at school can become utterly miserable through the comments and actions of others. The second part of the exercise allows children to articulate what they could do to make the class/lesson/break-time a happier experience.

It is worth noting that despite being what some readers may feel is a primary school-based activity, this exercise has proven successful in large secondary schools and specialist provision, as well as in primary schools. When bringing the activity to a close it is perhaps worth noting that:

- The members of staff at the end of the exercise are more confident and competent to teach all children and especially those who can be the most challenging.
- In the first instance developing effective work in behaviour means starting in the staffroom, not the classroom. This is not because that is where blame lies, but where our hopes must be.

When introducing **systemic theory** I start off with a challenge: that the group will be familiar with a key technique – **re-framing** – within the first five minutes. It runs as follows:

Step 1: Ask the group what behaviour most winds them up, compiling a list on a flipchart. Invariably the suggestions reflect the Elton research findings: high-frequency low-level disruptions, talking out of turn, wandering around, ignoring the teacher, chattering etc. (1 minute)

Step 2: Ask the group to work in pairs and to make notes on this next stage. They are asked to focus on one of the behaviours listed and respond to the following question:

- What possible benefits might the behaviour have for the pupil?

Or, a variation:

- What possible, legitimate reasons might there be for the behaviour?

The emphasis is on the positive dimension of the behaviour and the extent of possibility – colleagues do not have to arrive at a single reason. The aim here is to break thinking free of standard cause and effect theory. (2 minutes)

Step 3: Remaining in pairs, colleagues are now asked to review their list and cite a strategy for the pupil based on each of the possible explanations. They may draw on their own experience or consider something entirely off the wall. Once again, the aim is to encourage colleagues to respond creatively to difficulty. (2 minutes)

The same exercise can be used over a longer period of time as part of a more detailed use of the re-framing technique and if so the written notes can provide a valuable school compendium of actual and potential strategies for dealing with difficulty.

Another exercise that generates systemic thinking among colleagues is to introduce the concepts of deviant provocative and deviant insulative teaching. The idea is taken from the work of Chris Watkins and Patsy Wagner (Watkins and Wagner 2000) and often provides a light-hearted lead into some serious issues around teacher behaviour. Working on the basis that teachers find themselves behaving differently with different groups of pupils, the authors offer a continuum with deviance provocative and deviance insulative teaching at opposite ends. Descriptors for each type of teaching and possible questions for colleagues to discuss are presented in Figure 3.1.

Deviance provocative	Deviance insulative
Belief that pupils defined as deviant do not want to work and will do anything to avoid work.	Belief that pupils really want to work.
Impossible to provide conditions for pupils to work so pupils must change.	Conditions are assumed to be at fault.
Disciplinary interactions are a contest or battle which the teacher must win.	Disciplinary interactions relate to a clear set of classroom rules which are made explicit to pupils.
Teacher is unable to defuse situations and becomes involved in confrontations.	Teacher allows pupils to 'save face' and avoid confrontations.
Beliefs and values which feed a vicious cycle where behaviour does not go well.	Beliefs and values which feed a virtuous cycle where behaviour goes well.

Where do we find ourselves operating as provocative?

Where do we find ourselves acting as insulative?

With which groups of pupils or individuals?
At what times, in which curriculum areas, parts of the building/grounds?
What leads to it happening?

(Adapted from Watkins and Wagner 2000)

Figure 3.1 Deviance provocative and deviance insulative teaching

The emphasis in this exercise is on encouraging staff to identify with differences in the type of *teaching* they use with pupils. It is important that it is not regarded as an activity through which *teachers* are categorised! The systemic point to be made is that a range of factors impact on how individuals behave and engage with others and that combinations of factors change, as does the behaviour of all parties.

Throughout my work with staff groups the emphasis is on teachers becoming critically aware of the potential and limitations of particular theories and related techniques. Making the point that neither children nor teachers fail in classrooms, but systems and theory fail us, is a good place both to start, and close, a training session.

Ideas for working in a multi-agency environment

Over the past couple of years there has been a tremendous growth in multi-agency collaboration in terms of policy-making and practice. Since the late

1990s there has been a great deal of activity generated by a range of different combinations of cross-professional projects. The requirement for areas to have a Youth Offender Team (YOT) was arguably the most significant development leading to multi-professional interventions. There have also been a number of initiatives aimed at promoting similar work, including:

- refocusing the work of Child and Adolescent Mental Health Service (CAMHS);
- guidance for the education of children in public care;
- the national review of the youth service and Connexions strategy;
- the remit of the newly formed Children and Young People's Unit;
- the Quality Protects agenda for local social service departments.

The list is not exhaustive; there have been dozens of locally funded programmes focusing on joint working by agencies, in addition to a further cluster of initiatives delivered by the voluntary sector.

It has only been over the past couple of years that a more radical dimension of multi-agency intervention has emerged in mainstream educational thinking.

> ...education and teachers alone cannot compensate for society... [B. Bernstein argues] that all too often schools are expected to overcome problems of poverty, under-achievement and disruptive behaviour...This [is] unrealistic and the key to resolving some of these deep-rooted issues was inter-professional partnerships and inter-agency collaboration. It must be emphasised that this approach cannot be seen as an option for professionals. (Hamill and Boyd 2001)

More recently there has been a more explicit connection made between the inter-agency intervention and the realisation of social inclusion. At its more radical level this can mean schools becoming a platform for delivering a range of welfare services including community health, youth work and social worker input.

It used to be the case and in many places remains so that teachers would understandably complain of being expected to be social workers. In some areas new developments are taking place that in effect break the personnel monopoly that teachers once had in schools. In other words social work is being delivered in schools, but by social workers, youth workers are providing youth work and health professionals are delivering health care. Some work has already gone on that explores where schools have begun to shape themselves as a hub for delivering community services (see Klein 1999) and an emerging recognition of the child protection role that school can have for youngsters (see Gilligan 1998).

There have been examples of exciting and effective practice around the country where practitioners from different professional stables have met to tackle common challenges. Perhaps not surprisingly there have been a series of concerns that have also emerged. The National Foundation for Education Research (NFER) carried out a local study of multi-agency work aimed at primary school intervention in North East Lincolnshire LEA and identified a number of successful outcomes that are arguably typical of similar projects elsewhere (Haynes 1999):

- the development of 'new awareness' about children;
- where teachers had seen the team in action they were motivated to try out new ideas;
- changes in teachers' practice where they had the opportunity for feedback and where the activity had been supported by the school;
- enabling personal and social developmental issues to be addressed;
- a major impact on the professional development of team members.

The refreshing combination of insights into children's needs and the potential for staff development is a substantial advantage to pursuing multi-agency work. It is also a reliable avenue for developing systemic behaviour support. Through drawing in social workers, psychologists and youth workers to focus on a common objective in the school context, re-framing situations becomes an integral strand to the work.

However, as many services are realising, the pressure to work in collaboration with other teams can create difficulties. The NFER study identified a number of general factors that can threaten successful multi-professional practice, some of which included:

- coordination between agencies and local projects in how they work with local schools;
- consistency of team members in terms of how their time is allocated to joint work;
- clarity regarding the line management of the team and the team manager;
- consensus across strategic line managers about the approaches to be used;
- raising awareness of heads and teachers about the value and impact of multi-agency approaches;
- adequate resourcing for the support team.

In addition, behaviour support services have identified more specific factors that can get in the way of establishing good working relations with other teams:

- *Different, competing service priorities.* Where the behaviour support service is intending to facilitate staff development this can be seen to clash with, for example, a social service team that is primarily interested in securing direct support for a child.
- *Different concepts about who is to benefit from the intervention.* A familiar line is that the teacher uses the term 'pupil', social worker 'client' and health professional 'patient'. Each label carries a meaning about respective professional purpose and attitude and in practice these differences can also lead to contrary working practices.

Arguably the most successful multi-agency work has taken place where colleagues from different teams focus on common interests and needs, where there is comprehensive and transparent initial contracting and where each partner is able to make a distinctive contribution to a task. The following case studies illustrate how LEA behaviour support services have provided a platform for school-based multi-professional intervention.

Case study: Finding common ground

In this case an LEA behaviour support service had become increasingly frustrated in engaging with the local mental health specialist service. The support teachers were frequently coming across individual cases in desperate need of specialist intervention but were frequently told that waiting lists for appointments were measured in months. Even where work was being carried out, little if any feedback was being provided from the specialist to education partners. Several schools reflected a similar experience and there had been little hope of any collaborative work.

By introducing systemic re-framing, possibilities started to emerge. Mental health specialists felt increasingly paralysed by the overwhelming demand for individual work and had begun considering ways of further limiting access to the service. Their sense of frustration was heightened in the light of recent guidance encouraging mental health services to focus on early intervention and enskilling other 'frontline professionals'. The sense of isolation of the mental health team only served to maintain a key target professional group at arm's length. In other words, it became more helpful to perceive the mental health team as highly motivated to work differently but hemmed in by the expectations of other agencies.

A subsidiary issue was the apparent difficulty in schools getting any information from the service. Education agencies, with only a peripheral involvement with mental health specialists, tended to assume that the intervention was aimed at resolving school-based difficulties. In the majority of instances this was rarely the case; outstanding difficulties regarding family, welfare and medical issues were more often the determining reasons for the referral and focus of work. Furthermore, the specialists often only had access to the family to carry out the work on the basis of a confidentiality that was determined by the family. Consequently it was rarely possible for the specialist to divulge any details (unless expressly permitted by the family), as they had no authority to do so.

In developing collaborative work between the behaviour support service, mental health teams and schools it was necessary to re-frame established perceptions. First, the behaviour support team could present itself as a channel through which preventative work and training could be brokered. The service offered a golden opportunity for mental health specialists to access the universal context of schools. Second, the behaviour support team needed to accept that pursuing individual referrals for full support was simply inviting the mental health team into work they could not afford to take on. Third, it was not helpful to insist on receiving information from colleagues who were not able to provide it. Consequently a series of activities were planned and delivered that proved to be both exciting and engaging for all parties.

Team supervision: the mental health team allocated time to provide the support service with group supervision on a half-termly basis. These half-day sessions could be used to share particularly difficult casework or thematic concerns. The aim was for the specialist to support and help the behaviour support team to reflect on situations and consider possible strategies. It was not primarily a mechanism for presenting referrals.

The sessions proved invaluable in terms of building greater trust between the teams and raising awareness of a) the very valuable skills of therapists and b) the highly challenging work being tackled by the support service.

Transition work: in its work with schools the behaviour support service ran a series of group sessions for vulnerable pupils in preparation for phase transition. It was clear that the input would include handling closure and change, both of which presented particular sensitivities for the group. The social worker from the mental health team was made available to work with both the pupils and their parents in planning for transition. Once again it provided an opportunity to make available specialist input without the need for referral while making a valuable contribution to an education programme.

Case study: Joining the party

In the same LEA featured above, the popularity of the joint work with the mental health team led to a wider collaborative initiative involving other agencies, including the local family health centre and education welfare service. The behaviour support service partnership planned a series of sessions for parents of nursery-aged children preparing to move into reception. Parents and carers whose first child was moving up to school were asked to identify the themes that they most wanted support on. The responses formed the basis of a loosely structured agenda for a series of sessions, hosted by the school, coordinated by the support service and delivered by colleagues from the various agencies. Topics for discussion included managing tantrums, eating and sleeping difficulties, the importance of play, special needs, attendance and general child development. The programme was run at a number of local schools and arrangements differed each time given the demands of parents. Refreshments were offered and in some cases a crèche was provided for the duration of sessions.

The school was able to access parents and prepare them fully for the change to school routines, while the individual agencies valued the access to families who might never be referred but welcomed support at a lighter level of engagement.

In both this and the previous case study, it became clear that collaboration was not going to happen while agencies focused only on where they differed or on delivering impossible tasks. Instead, seeking out common agendas and recognising the unique contributions of each partner were much more productive factors.

Case study: Joint solution building

In another LEA the local primary behaviour support service was increasingly concerned with a core group of referrals where there was a range of home-related concerns. Early discussion with the local family centre established that the therapists and social workers in that team also shared several of the cases. The family centre team was working with families in isolation from behaviour support team members, who were focusing on school-based concerns.

Following a series of partnership planning meetings a multi-layered strategy was set up that included professionals from each team jointly running group work for children in schools, sessions for parents of the children at other venues and providing feedback to schools involved. The work with children included a degree of therapeutic intervention while the parent-focused input took the form of informal training and self-help group work.

The process challenged many of the preconceptions among professionals and sharpened awareness of respective working practices. Most importantly though, the exercise was the first local example of where professionals from across health, social services and education teams were involved in delivering support to families and children.

Case study: Youth workers – a school's ace card

Until a couple of years ago the idea of deploying youth workers in schools was considered something that was toyed with back in the 1970s and something not to be repeated. Numerous schools with adjacent youth club provision had disassociated themselves with the unfair, archetypal image of pool, raffia work and table tennis. However, youth work in education is enjoying a renaissance, and not before time.

A behaviour support service in south London started employing youth workers as part of its core team in the 1990s. The role of the workers covered a combination of the following tasks:

- Contribute to running group work for pupils and leading specific sessions.
- Directly support especially vulnerable pupils at risk of exclusion or non-attendance.
- Provide support to pupils with Statements of Special Educational Needs.
- Contribute to the training of lunch-time supervisors in relation to leading play activities.

The service quickly began to appreciate the distinct contribution that youth workers can bring to the work of schools. In the past, for instance, pupils with Statements of SEN had been allocated either additional teacher or learning assistant time. For most pupils this combination was satisfactory, but for a small vulnerable minority who tended to experience exclusions and non-attendance, this approach to additional support proved ineffective. The main reason for this was that both teachers and LSAs tended to be solely school-based. The professional upbringing of these groups is based on the assumption that they can provide support when the pupil attends, which is fine unless, of course, the neediest pupils also happen to be the most absent! Youth workers have a quite different professional pedigree and are arguably more comfortably deployed outside of the classroom and into corridors, school grounds, the streets and ultimately back at the youngster's home. It is no exaggeration to describe the impact of effective youth work by adapting a well-known advertising slogan:

'Youth workers reach the parts other professionals don't.'

Similarly in deploying youth workers in school-based youth work, young people responded well to the additional, distinct voice. Nowadays many colleagues with a background in youth work have found themselves employed as mentors – either as part of local youth service initiatives or as Learning Support Mentors under the Excellence in Cities programme. This work involves providing support to individual children and in some more advanced examples, delivering alternative curriculum programmes.

At a number of schools based in south Wales, youth workers have been employed to develop alternative curriculum programmes at Key Stage 3. This has included introducing pre-vocational training experiences, residential trips, accredited extra-curricular activities and structured group work, in addition to support for individual children. In each school the work is coordinated by a teacher from the pastoral team who also shares in delivering some of the programme, but for the most part the youth worker is responsible for the day-to-day running of the sessions.

In some services and schools a number of concerns are raised about the potential use of a youth worker, most of which are around the difficulties in what is referred to as the youth worker's 'informal' approach. Teachers have suspicions about the worker becoming too much the friend of the young person, or even more so, an advocate. There has been some early anecdotal evidence of where Learning Support Mentors have become especially protective in the classroom of how a teacher has reprimanded a supported youngster and clearly the potential divisiveness of such situations is unsustainable in the school context.

The most crucial factor for ensuring effective youth work in schools lies entirely in the initial contracting process. Before youth workers and teachers work directly with young people it is critical that there is clarity and consensus on what the role entails and what it does *not* include. Problems arise where the role of the youth worker is poorly explained to staff, professional vulnerabilities are exploited when there is confusion about responsibilities and resentment follows where potential professional jealousies are not addressed before work starts.

Case study: Doing time

In another LEA the behaviour support service has a close association with the local youth offender team (YOT). There was often informal contact between team members but little direct joint work, until a particularly difficult referral. A Year 11 male pupil at a school had been convicted of a burglary at the home of a younger female pupil at the same school. Understandably the parents of the girl were angry that the boy would be attending the school with their daughter fearing that since his conviction he might intimidate the girl, and they urged the head teacher to exclude the boy. The head teacher was sympathetic to the parents' view but was keenly aware that the offence had no connection with the boy's placement and also knew that the boy's continued attendance at the school could well present ongoing difficulties.

The boy had been referred to the support service some months prior to the offence and his placement at the school had been relatively stable. However, the support teacher doubted that she could continue to support him sufficiently given the heightened concerns about his placement, which were beginning to impact on the boy's attitude to school.

Meanwhile, the allocated YOT keyworker had been anxious to avoid a custodial sentence for the boy, whose offending record had been previously low key. Consequently in presenting a pre-sentence report to the court the keyworker had emphasised the improved situation at school in terms of the boy's behaviour and engagement with his studies. The court issued an intensive supervision order.

So, the support teacher had a case that she felt was beginning to get beyond her expertise; the head teacher was feeling increasingly like King Solomon, with the parents of the younger pupil demanding exclusion and/or increased monitoring of the boy; while the YOT keyworker had cited the improved school situation as an important positive factor in the boy's current situation.

The eventual response was perhaps the only way of making good out of extremely difficult circumstances, but it also gave rise to a very powerful piece of work. An unorthodox decision was taken for alternate supervision order sessions to take place in school, thereby increasing the amount of in-school support for the boy but also demonstrating to the girl's parents that the school took their concerns seriously. The boy knew that to breach a supervision order would bring his case back to court, a situation that he wanted to avoid now that he was 'straightening himself out'. The YOT were able to keep close contact with the school and the behaviour support teacher continued in providing the pupil with educational support. The head teacher demonstrated a considerable degree of patience and a very tangible commitment to meeting needs of all pupils under exceptional pressure. The girl and her parents also felt that their concerns had been genuinely respected and that they had been supported during a stressful period.

Following on from this unconventional but successful intervention the support service and the YOT ran a two-day programme for pastoral care staff in raising awareness of the youth justice system. This was jointly delivered by senior YOT practitioners and the behaviour support team and involved a visit to a regional young offenders' institute, an experience that had a profound impact on the year heads' appreciation of why school was so important for the most challenging of young people.

Delivering effective behaviour support: pupil-based intervention

As discussed in the opening section of this book, effective behaviour support cannot rely solely on intervening at the level of school or staff development. Children bring rich resources and challenges to the classroom and how adults respond within the context of the organisation significantly determines the extent to which problem situations develop. Inevitably the work of the BST will involve a degree of detailed intervention at the level of the individual pupil, and the extent to which this represents a large or small caseload will in turn depend on the organisational behaviour of the support service.

This section is not intended to provide a comprehensive guide to working with children. There is already a wide range of resources of this type to support the work of behaviour support specialists (see, for example, the listings of Lucky Duck Publishing, Smallwood Publishing or Incentive Plus distribution). Instead this section offers guidance notes for delivering support to individual pupils within the context of a systemic approach, details for operating a local exclusion hotline and some pointers for reintegrating pupils into a new placement.

Managing individual casework

Regardless of the approach used by the behaviour support service, there are some common dilemmas in working with individual pupils:

- balancing boundaries, e.g. professional and personal involvement, service remit and the remit of other agencies;
- time-limiting involvement, ensuring that the support teacher has the capacity to take on the next referral;
- fear of what will happen if we do not pursue the case, e.g. will the support service withdrawal result in exclusion, family breakdown, care placement change?
- closing the case with confidence that the school will be able to sustain the improvement;
- providing the right level of support/time/type of support;
- avoiding dependency of the child, family, school;
- fear of de-skilling as opposed to en-skilling schools;
- continuing to remind schools of their 'contract' with the support teacher and the child;
- clarifying roles (especially with regard to the deployment of behaviour support service assistants);
- working within an LEA context and responding to school-identified needs.

This list alone indicates why external agencies need to take great care prior to becoming involved in individual casework. A prerequisite for casework is a conscious realisation by the support teacher that such dilemmas exist. One of the most worrying situations that can emerge is where, through inadequate induction and poor supervision, individual members of the team continue to work with children and families with little awareness of the emotional implications of casework. A consequence of this situation is that dependency issues can become established which then make for difficulty in maintaining systemic support.

Individual work can emerge for a number of reasons and it is important to recognise that there can be a range of objectives for the service getting involved, including a combination of the following.

There is a combination of aims which differ from case to case but include the following possibilities:

- To contribute to an assessment of a child's needs.
- To explore and develop potential solutions to problem behaviour.
- To enhance the child's experience of school.
- To maintain the child within the community of the school.
- To develop inclusive provision for children with behavioural difficulties.
- To enable the school to achieve effective work with the pupil.
- To work in collaboration with other agencies in meeting a pupil's needs.

Some pointers worth considering regarding individual work are presented in Figure 3.2. They were included in guidance for a behaviour support service working in a county LEA in the west of England.

- **Establish as soon as possible the school's commitment and motivation to the child's placement**

    This has been an area in which the support teacher can feel 'ambushed' by discovering that the school's intentions have been to discharge the pupil in some way and that their involvement is part of the process of exclusion or shifting the youngster into a specialist placement:
    - Try to expose and explore the full range of school perspectives of the child and work with the differing viewpoints (the Towards Better Behaviour model is useful in doing this, see Chapter 2).
    - Pursue links with other agencies and parents – do not rely on the school to have done so.

- **Change takes time**

    The school may not appreciate that the process of change takes time and may be eager to dismiss intervention because improvements are not rapid.
    - Flag this point up at the outset, be conservative with forecasting changes (remember the psychological contracting principle, see Chapter 2).
    - Encourage reflection – not reaction.

Figure 3.2 Working with individuals: Golden Rules

- **Boundaries versus responsibilities**

  The behaviour support teacher needs to be clear with him/herself and others – parent/carer, school, pupil – about what they are responsible for. Invariably it is far less than imagined! (Remember the process contracting principle in Chapter 2.)

- **Endeavour to dispel the myths**

  This relates to the complex business of reminding schools why they exist and setting out how support service intervention is linked to fulfilling the *school's* aims. It also relates to making it clear that exclusion is rarely a helpful solution and does not make things any easier for the child.
  - A key question in this situation is less about what the school wants, but more about what the child needs.

- **Do not underestimate the potential difficulties of complex cases**

  Those cases where a number of agencies are involved tend to be those that remain open longest. Remain clear-sighted regarding the 'value added' dimension of service involvement (see point below).

- **Keep the case as simple as it needs to be**

  Do not rely on the involvement of other agencies to make things easier – unless of course it is simply a business of brokering a referral to another service, as opposed to joint working the case. It is rarely the case that joint working makes resolution swifter.

- **Light touch networking**

  Do not be afraid to say no when it is clear that too many agencies have already said yes. Ask the question: What is it that is so special about behaviour support intervention that it is worth offering? Remember, it might be more appropriate to suggest that agencies already on the case work more effectively rather than involve us and complicate matters further.

- **Take the minimalist approach**

  Ask a few basic questions before leaving the office to 'do' a case:
  - Why am I going?
  - What do I hope to get out of the visit/meeting?
  - Is what I am about to do going to reinforce or distort my role in relation to the case?
        If we don't have clear answers to these, don't go!
  - Do we need to know everything about the child, family and peers to deliver effective intervention? Go only as far as we need to meet the objectives for the work; anything more confuses others regarding our role and can be little more than interference.
  - If the school says it can now manage then leave the case alone – with the proviso that the support service is available at the end of the phone.
        If in doubt – don't go out!

Figure 3.2 continued

Operating an exclusion hotline

For many behaviour specialists working in LEA services an inevitable expectation will be that support can be offered at times of crisis and particularly when exclusion is imminent. Behaviour support service responses to these calls for support are notoriously difficult for a number of reasons:

- LEA officers will tend to assume that the service can, and will, resolve what are often highly complex cases.
- Head teachers will be working under significant pressure and will expect a swift and effective resolution, or
- Head teachers will be seeking to involve the service in order to legitimise exclusion.
- The pupil and their family may have very strong views about the situation which in turn present difficulties when negotiating options.
- Other parties including class teachers, professional associations and parents of other pupils may also be lobbying for exclusion.

Responding from a systemic perspective in these situations is without doubt an extremely subtle and diplomatic process. In some instances the pupil at risk may already be known to the service. However, it can often be the case that the child is an unknown entity, committed a 'one-off' serious offence and now faces a long-term exclusion.

There have been a small number of examples of where a local behaviour support service has established a hotline service for managing crisis situations. During the early 1990s Staffordshire LEA operated a hotline as part of a short-term-funded initiative. Due to a reduction in anticipated resources, the support service was unable to provide a wide coverage of peripatetic support. The hotline service became the main channel for generating the limited available support. In 1996, following the Staffordshire experiment, Merton BSS in south London set up a similar arrangement and this work is covered in the case study below.

Case study: Generating second chances

The Merton model occurred by chance. A head teacher took the decision to permanently exclude a Year 7 child, informed the parents and had verbally agreed the decision with the governing body and was preparing the relevant paperwork.

By chance the head teacher met the head of behaviour support in passing and mentioned how sad she was at having had to exclude a child with such a high level of need. The service had not worked with the youngster and the head of service was curious about how the head teacher had arrived at such a dramatic decision. It became clear that she was under tremendous pressure from a number of staff and was also aware that the pupil's class teacher had

---

been experiencing difficulties with the whole class. Things had become more tricky in the past few days as a number of the class were really pushing the teacher's limits. It was nearly the end of term and the head teacher just felt that she had had enough, something had to give and the pupil gave her an opportunity to take a stance by becoming abusive to the member of staff.

Over a brief discussion the head teacher recognised that the decision to permanently exclude was probably not the most useful response to a complex situation and would not resolve an underlying issue of improving the class teacher's relationship with pupils. However, in the middle of all the competing pressures and demands, the head teacher had found it difficult to keep a strategic perspective. The outcome of the conversation was that a short fixed-term exclusion was given, the service supported the reintegration of the pupil and perhaps most significantly, partnership planned support for the class teacher.

In the end the support for the pupil became merged into the class-based partnership plan. His placement was sustained for the remainder of his time at the school and the class work involved piloting strategies that were integrated in whole-school policy. So, for example, the individual child's behaviour was associated with a generally inconsistent use of praise as a rule reinforcer in the class. By focusing on using rule-related praise with all pupils in the class, in addition to the introduction of class-based 'Golden Time' (a once-a-week period of free choice for pupils earned through good behaviour), significant progress was made in the behaviour of the whole group. As a result of this success the work was disseminated to all staff to form a wider school approach.

On reflection it became clear that only by chance had a permanent exclusion been avoided. How many other permanent exclusions might have been avoided had the head teacher had an opportunity to talk through a current difficult scenario? It was at this point that the service learnt of the Staffordshire initiative and began to plan a local version of the exclusion hotline. In this instance, the hotline added to what was already a wide range of intervention including individual referrals, consultancy and project work. Consequently the following criteria were used in presenting the hotline which had a dedicated phone number:

- It was for head teacher use only (or acting head teacher) – the service already had entry points for other staff.
- It was for use *only* when a pupil was at risk of *permanent* exclusion – the aim of this intervention was purely to reduce permanent exclusions; where concerns were anything less than crisis, other routes into the service were encouraged.

On the basis of local exclusion data it was anticipated that the hotline would not be heavily used – there were at most 40 permanent exclusions the previous year. However, it was also understood that when the phone rang the call was going to need sensitive handling. A letter was circulated to all head teachers providing details of the service and guaranteeing a response by the end of the working day and appropriate action within a maximum of two days. It was decided that the service was promoted as a 'hotline' as opposed to a 'helpline' to emphasise the urgency of exclusion scenarios and avoid accentuating a sense of vulnerability on behalf of the school.

A series of guidance notes were provided for those members of the service who took calls and these are provided below in Figure 3.3. Blank crib sheets were used for the support teacher to make notes and provide an aide memoire during the call and when completed kept in a central hotline file. The process notes give an overview of how calls were dealt with. All calls were logged to build a profile of hotline use and this included call 'disposals'. This generated interesting evaluative data with most calls in the first year not requiring any further action. In several instances it was necessary to set up individual support programmes, while in others the outcome was to set up a partnership planning meeting to arrange project work.

Hot Line Crib Sheet

Guidelines

The following pointers are by no means exhaustive – you may need to explore responses through further questioning not detailed here.

- Try to avoid shooting questions at the caller – it is preferable to elicit the information without direct questioning.
- The purpose of the hotline is to allow the caller to talk through the issues, not for us to talk them through what we think.
- Use the following table to make notes – if you use anything else, staple it to this sheet.

The call

Head teacher: **School:**

Pupil name: **Year:**

Details of the specific incident

- Is the above part of a pattern?
- Who else was involved?
- What might the trigger have been?
- How are others feeling at the moment, i.e. staff, pupils, parents?

- Where *exactly* are we in terms of the exclusion process, i.e. has the letter gone out?
- What contact/relationship has there been with the parent/carer prior to the incident?
- Who at school has maintained these contacts?
- What other agencies have been involved?
- Which agencies are *currently* involved?
- Has/is social services involved?
- Where *exactly* is the pupil in terms of SEN stage and/or Pastoral Support Planning?

Figure 3.3 Exclusion hotline materials

- Where does the pupil live, i.e. are they out of borough?
- What year group is the pupil?
- What is the pupil's ethnicity?
- What has worked in the past?
- What does the head teacher want to happen now?
- Arrange visit time (must be within three working days).

Internal Behaviour Support Team Discussion

The key role of the support team in reflecting on the call is to:

- derive the best possible solution;
- generate back-up option(s);
- prevent the possible crisis of the exclusion overshadowing the search for a solution.

An important task is to *clarify at the outset* the role of the behaviour support teacher and to identify exactly *who* is to be involved in the case.

There are clearly numerous variables for each case and it is not practical to try and define every possible response. However, in discussing a case the following broad considerations might be made:

- Is a partnership planning exercise the most useful (and sole) intervention?
- Would it help to free the class teacher up for half a day as part of the above?
- Would a network meeting – arranged by the support teacher – be the most efficient means of planning an intervention?
- Is the central difficulty a breakdown in home-school relations; is this where our efforts ought to be directed?
- Do we need to be more directly involved?
- Is the pupil already an individual referral?
- Would counselling be most appropriate?
- Is there a need for a team behaviour support assistant input?

It is anticipated that the intervention will be clearly stipulated to the school and will be reviewed regularly. In cases where direct assistant support is being used there needs to be a fortnightly review with a maximum period of intervention of six weeks/half a term.

Notes:

1. A possible outcome may be that the head teacher will feel sufficiently supported and advised as a result of the initial phone call. It may not always be necessary to make a follow-up visit.
2. Fixed-term rather than permanent exclusion to be recommended as first course of action.
3. It is not necessary – or possibly advisable – for the support teacher to be involved in the re-entry interview.

Figure 3.3 continued

At the end of the first year there had been a total of 19 calls regarding pupils who were being considered for permanent exclusion. Only four of these cases went on to be permanently excluded. It is worth noting that during that same year there were just over 30 permanent exclusions from LEA schools. As a result of the hotline service the following observations were made:

- In many instances when a head teacher has made their decision to exclude they tend not to be open to considering an alternative option, or seek an external perspective.
- When head teachers decide to seek an opportunity to reflect on a crisis situation via a hotline, in the majority of cases permanent exclusion is avoided.

Informal feedback from head teachers indicated that for many the experience of permanently excluding a pupil was an extremely painful and lonely one – an aspect that is rarely acknowledged by other parties. The opportunity to talk through scenarios was both highly valued by individual head teachers but also safeguarded vulnerable pupils.

4 Monitoring and evaluation

This section considers possible approaches to monitoring and evaluation and addresses common dilemmas and questions. Delivering effective behaviour support based on a systemic model makes particular demands on measuring and reviewing success. What follows are examples of how support services have innovated conventional monitoring and evaluation to take into account the impact of support on school systems and culture.

Service evaluation is a theme that has only been seriously addressed by services over the last few years. In the past the concept of evaluating behaviour support was at best an afterthought. In most cases behaviour support, as with other specialist support work, remained outside the increasingly rigorous framework for monitoring schools' performance. An earlier tendency was for services to assume that as long as schools remained generally happy with support arrangements there was little to worry about and the success of support generally relied on maintaining the placements of individual children. There is little evidence that many services were involved in detailed monitoring and evaluation during the early 1990s, and nothing pre-1990. This was an era when LEA support services enjoyed a role untouched by the threat of Fair Funding and the increased autonomy of schools. Consequently the pressure to demonstrate value for money, accountability and progress against performance indicators and local targets was absent.

Behaviour support has been evaluated in some LEAs and in a few cases material has been made available to a wider audience through regional dissemination and specialist journals (see for example, Leggett 2000). The work of Merton LEA's Attendance and Behaviour Support Service (ABSS) was featured in DfEE guidance for drafting LEA Behaviour Support Plans and was the focus for a report published by the Centre for Studies in Inclusive Education (CSIE) (Barrow 1998). Attempts were also made by the DfEE to collate evaluation summaries of individual government-funded projects, although this came to a halt at the end of the yearly funded programmes operating during the 1990s.

Perhaps the only report that offers a consideration of behaviour support can be found within the DfEE evaluation report on the impact of a three-year government-funded programme aimed at reducing exclusion (Hallam and Castle 1999). It is a significant report and one associated with a degree of controversy for those involved in behaviour support. The government relied heavily on the report at regional conferences in justifying its development of the now widespread policy to set up Learning Support Units under the Excellence in Cities programme. It was argued that the evaluation team, based at the Institute of Education, London, had identified that on-site provision was both more effective in preventing exclusion and had cost benefit advantages over placements in Pupil Referral Units. However, what officials omitted to say was that the report identified that the most effective means of preventing exclusion at the most efficient cost was through the work of multi-professional behaviour support services. Unfortunately such a finding was not going to win political support at a time when the push to delegate further money from LEAs to schools was – and remains – such a high priority.

Despite all the activity on measuring performance, both of schools and pupils, there is no available established model for behaviour support services. In the absence of an evaluation framework several services have begun to use operational data, for example rates of case referrals and outcomes, to assess performance. While any move towards a more rigorous review process is to be welcomed, some reservations need to be raised. Often locally determined indicators can mean little more than meeting truancy and exclusion targets – both of which are by implication pupil-orientated. Operational data can also tend to include only input information leading to assessments about the varying level of support provided to individual schools. Detail about how many visits and hours the service has delivered to children are provided and often it is possible to provide a profile of the range of children supported. In terms of delivering a systemic model of support, these approaches to service evaluation can only ever be a small part of the process.

Monitoring and evaluating systemic support

One of the first principles to establish in developing an evaluation framework is that any method must reflect the values and intentions of the behaviour support model. In other words, if the service is aiming to change school culture and levels of teacher confidence and competence then service evaluation should be centred on these aspects. The tendency to focus on child-based indicators such as attendance and exclusion rates are only of partial value when considering the impact of systems-orientated support.

One of the first tasks of the support team is to establish the aims and objectives that are at the heart of the service. Where these are explicitly linked to changes in staff attitude and whole-school approach, extensive consideration needs to be given to identifying alternative indicators for success and ways of measuring a wider range of input and process information. If we refer to conventional monitoring and evaluation methodology the tendency will be to focus on pupil-based information, as presented in Figure 4.1. The service can use a number of data sources to build a full picture of how it has been successful in working with individual children over a given period. However, this method provides little insight into how the behaviour support has impacted on the context within which the child's behaviour was seen as problematic. This is the most crucial missing link when working systemically.

Type of data	Description	Source
Input and referral	• Number of visits and hours per child, including preparatory and direct inputs • Profile of referral cohort including age, year group, ethnicity, care status, SEN, address etc. • Indication of reason for referral/difficulty • Profile of other agencies involved	• Service referral pro formas • Service casework files • School pupil file • Assessment records
Process	• Quality of support offered to the child and/or family • Perception of child, staff, parents regarding support	• Case study material • IEP records • Questionnaire • Interviews
Outcomes	• Reduction in exclusion • Increased attendance • Sustained placement • Increased stability re: care placement • Reduction in SEN stage • Increased self-esteem • Decreased internal/school-based sanctions • Increased achievement • Total summative closure details for pupil cohort	• School pupil file • Whole-school data • Service casework file • Service case closure records • Assessment record

Figure 4.1 Conventional monitoring and evaluation information

If we want to make headway in evaluating systemic support the emphasis must be on tracking a wider range of potential factors and performance indicators. Some early consideration of this was offered by Rennie and his work provides a helpful overview of this need to widen the remit of behaviour support evaluation (Rennie 1993). One way of generating useful ideas and early plans is a team-based exercise based on the following discussion points:

• If we are committed as a team to bringing about systemic change what would this look like in terms of service activity?
• How would we know that we had made a difference to how staff and schools work regarding behaviour?
• In terms of input, what would a pie-chart look like at the end of a year's operation? How would it be sliced: 50% staff and school development, 50% individual referral? Or a different combination?
• What information about the school behaviour might we want to monitor and evaluate?
• More specifically, if we have work linked to individual classes, or members of staff or whole-school development, what might be the respective success indicators?

As a consequence of these discussions a team is encouraged to reaffirm and clarify service aims but also to begin to articulate the intended difference it can make to schools, staff and children within a framework of systemic values. The discussions are firmly rooted in a perspective that discourages a preoccupation with solely pupil-based evaluation. A more comprehensive range of information reflecting an holistic evaluation of behaviour support is presented in Figure 4.2. What becomes clear is that the partnership planning process can be the most important channel for guiding and informing service monitoring and evaluation.

Type of information	Description	Source
Input and referral	• Profile of range of staff worked with, *i.e. % of SENCOs, Deputy Head, HOY/HOD, governors, LSAs etc.* • Range of intervention type, *i.e. group work, policy development, staff training* • Range of themes addressed, *i.e. bullying, race/gender harassment, anger management, emotional literacy, thinking skills, classroom management* • Source of referral, *i.e. school via development plan/OFSTED, LEA via school monitoring mechanism, other agency concern*	• Partnership plan • Casework file • LEA planning system • School development plan
Process	• Investigating the experience of staff being supported by the service • Canvassing the perceptions of BSS input by other agencies working with the school • Considering the perspective of appropriate LEA officers in terms of the BSS meeting LEA expectations	• Case study material • Questionnaire • Interviews • Partnership planning reviews
Outcome	• Decreased whole-school/group exclusion rates • Decreased whole-school/group truancy rates • Increased competency of staff • Increased sense of staff confidence • Greater development of LEA policy • Greater development of whole-school policy/approach	• Whole-school data • LEA-based data • Partnership planning reviews

Figure 4.2 Information for monitoring and evaluating systemic behaviour support

Evaluating and monitoring behaviour support: process

It is entirely intentional that at this point in this book I refer right back to the section on setting up work in the second chapter. One of the more important principles of the partnership planning process is identifying the purpose for the intervention and in doing so describing the intended gains to be had from doing the work. It is this part of the initial negotiations that is crucial for shaping evaluation and monitoring. For example, if group work is being planned for a dozen pupils it is vital that success criteria are agreed on prior to the work starting. It is these criteria that form the basis of reviewing and evaluating the work at closure. Deciding how to measure the success of a project at the *end* of the work is seriously flawed and allows for a number of errors. Colleagues can forget what the presenting difficulty was that prompted the work, expectations about what success might look like can have changed and unexpected activity that has emerged during the period can inadvertently become the focus for evaluation. Instead, sound partnership planning meetings should generate clear monitoring criteria that are SMART (Specific – Measurable – Achievable – Realistic – Time-limited).

The supervision of team managers needs to promote the use of the partnership planning process as an important evaluative exercise. In some services the partnership plan is the focus for casework supervision and guidance. In effect through reviewing partnership plans the team manager can be monitoring the developing workload of individual team members, identify where problems are emerging and gather important operational factors.

Dependent on the particular filing and data entry arrangements for services it is possible to knit together a series of data streams to create an efficient monitoring system. A possible model is presented in the case study below. Perhaps the most important priority is to ensure that whichever model is used for monitoring service delivery, it feeds directly into a wider approach to service evaluation. While this may be self-evident it is worth noting that in some instances a behaviour support service may want to evaluate its impact on school and staff change but belatedly realise that the only monitoring data available relates to pupil-based indicators.

Case study: It's a GAS – Capturing elusive soft outcome data

Completing a project can be a bitter-sweet experience. On the one hand there is a sense of satisfaction in finishing a job well done, while on the other there is the business of tying up loose ends and ensuring that the moment is marked for posterity. In general practice, reviewing projects can be a less precise art than initially negotiating work.

A key point to make is that by shifting away from working almost entirely with pupils, where success indicators are bound up within specific personalised targets, there is an increasing need to demonstrate the value of project work. The assumption here is that the principle of setting a review

---

date at the point of initial negotiation is both well established and practised. Failure to do so could lead to serious headaches as the project progresses, and raised eyebrows from team leaders and school managers.

Assume that the review date is set and the work is coming to an end. There is a desire on the behalf of the behaviour support teacher to take the glory and run, or bear the grimaces, accept defeat and hope someone else gets the next project at the school. Whichever way it goes, the review is the best opportunity to collate critical evaluative data. It is critical for two reasons; firstly, because without a firm statement of effectiveness, success remains an anecdotal, 'feel-good' concept which does not cut much ice and secondly, in the wider scheme of things, it is difficult to justify shifting to a systemic way of working which remains less quantifiable.

Achievement in project work is difficult to quantify. Reading ages and on-task behaviour are arguably simpler to ascertain, but the extent to which colleagues *feel* supported is a more tricky notion to put a figure on. Goal Attainment Scaling (GAS) can provide an extremely valuable way of generating meaningful data. It offers a means for rating individual goals. Readers will be familiar with questionnaires asking to rate, on a scale from 1 to 4, how strongly respondents view particular proposals, or their feelings on a given issue, for example. In the context of the behaviour support service a simple substitution is made for the success criteria agreed at the outset of the project.

Let us take a look at a common example of project work – introducing rules, rewards and sanctions through a team teaching approach. In negotiating the project the behaviour support teacher agreed a number of success criteria, some of which are easily measurable – such as an increase in on-task behaviour, or a reduction in recorded sanctions.

However, there are some indicators that are less quantifiable, for example the extent to which the class teacher has felt more confident in managing the class. This might be remedied by asking the teacher how they might rate the success on a scale from 1 to 4 and recording the rating on the review section. It is arguably worth setting a rate for each of the criteria, regardless of how quantifiable they might be. In addition to putting a figure on those difficult-to-get-to success measures, the process will also provide comprehensive descriptions of the overall rating of the service for specific targets.

A number of services have been GAS-marking success criteria, and an example of a completed proforma is presented in Figure 4.3. Services have identified a number of benefits:

- The process helps focus the minds of all parties on the anticipated outcomes of the work, often reminding them at the review stage of the initial purpose of the intervention.
- It makes the evaluation of softer outcomes more robust.
- It encourages schools to check out their expectations about realistic pace and extent of change.
- Over time and range of projects the process generates insights into which success criteria the behaviour team are most effective in achieving and success criteria where further development is needed.

Secondary Behaviour Support Team
PROJECT EVALUATION

NAME OF SCHOOL:						
PROJECT TITLE:	*Working with teachers*					

Goal Achievement Success Mark (GAS mark) (overall how do you feel about the success of the project)	(1) (very good)	2	3	4 (poor)	

SBST member(s) involved: **RW**	Evaluation completed by: **ST**

Details of Project

1. **Working collaboratively with ST to share good practice, improve classroom and behaviour management skills**
2. **To raise morale and confidence of ST**
3. **To improve behaviour of Year 10 class**

Success criteria	Result/criteria achieved?	GAS mark (optional)
Improvement of on task behaviour of 25%	Overall there was a significant improvement of the class. Certainly more work is achieved now than before, even when lessons are not as smooth as I would like them to be.	2/1
Upward trend of morale and confidence of teacher	This was really significant to me. I found Rachel's input invaluable in the sense that her close observations of the situation and her advice provided a real basis from which I could proceed to achieve better outcomes.	1
Increased positive referrals given to class of 25%	A much better balance now prevails between positive and negative referrals. Pupils on Stage 2 for Emotional/Behavioural reasons have responded well to the focus on the positive and the number of 'difficult' incidents is gradually decreasing.	2/1

Further work required? Yes/No	**Improvements**
Suggestions for follow on work:	Suggestions to improve the effectiveness of this project:
I felt that the de-briefing sessions were really helpful and that it would be good to try to maintain the momentum. I have therefore invited Rachel to observe and comment in a lesson after a half-term has elapsed. The papers/reports which Rachel has since sent me have been really useful and I feel that when I need to, I can refer to something which offers sound, practical suggestions. It is my intention to share these documents with other colleagues so a commonality of approach, especially with difficult pupils, is likely to produce more work and better morale/confidence.	I believe that the project is effective as it stands. The simplicity of the project is its strength. I wonder if some 'top-up' INSET every term or so would be worth trying; this could be broadened out to other colleagues. The idea of Team Members staying in touch with teachers by sending relevant reading materials is one which could be incorporated into the Project if it is not already done routinely.

Figure 4.3 Example of a completed proforma

• When carrying out a whole service evaluation it is possible to summarise all GAS marks and make general observations about the relative success the service is making in increasing staff confidence and competence supported by quantitative evidence.

A potential difficulty identified by services using the GAS mark approach has been that individual team members believe that the grading exercise relates to professional performance. This is a pitfall that can be avoided by managers being explicit at the outset about the service monitoring purpose behind the approach and through simply not using GAS mark data in supervision or the performance management process.

The GAS rating is specifically focused on certain criteria, for example the extent to which the member of staff feels more confident in managing a difficult pupil. There may be several criteria and each may have a different level recorded. The factors that can affect the rating will be rooted in both the school and behaviour circumstances and include staff absence, delayed timescales, availability of resources etc. This is an approach that is used primarily to assess which success criteria the service is most and least successful in achieving – it is not designed as a mechanism to rate the performance of staff. Team leaders are strongly advised to declare this when introducing the approach and in managing its implementation.

Case study: Monitoring

In one inner London LEA the support team delivered to both primary and secondary schools. The authority covered both urban and suburban areas and had been successful in reducing permanent exclusions. Within the service there was a well-established commitment to providing three levels of support: whole-school development, intervention with teachers and groups of pupils, and multi-professional support for individual children and families. The service used a partnership planning approach for all project-based work, which covered any interventions linked with school development, class and group work. In the case of individual referrals a referral format involving pre-support consultation and solution-focused techniques was used.

In terms of monitoring data the service maintained two spreadsheets which were updated on at least a monthly basis or at the point of case closure or referral. The first spreadsheet maintained data pertaining to individual pupil casework and generated profiles of the range of referrals, the referring agent and type of difficulty, input totals and the case outcome at closure. The second spreadsheet maintained details of project work and generated information about the type of staff involved, nature of intervention, input and outcome data. Examples of the spreadsheets are provided in Figures 4.4 and 4.5. In some LEAs the project-based database has additional fields for including details of the goal attainment ratings so that outcome data is recorded alongside project input and profile information.

School	Phase	Focus	Intervention	Start	Ant. end	Staff involved	End date	No. of hours	No. of visits
St Abbots Primary	F	B/A	Parent support YrR	1/4/96	1/7/96	CT	1/12/96	10	7
Canon Hill Park	F	B	Class support Yr2	1/3/96	1/6/96	CT	1/6/96	10	9
St Cuthbert's Middle	M	B	Whole-school policy	1/1/96	1/6/96	HOYS/DHT	1/7/96	21	16
Richard Hill High	S	A	Whole-school policy	1/4/95	1/7/96	DHT/CTs	1/7/96	6	2
Richard Hill High	All	D	Youth Justice	1/5/96	1/5/96	PSHE Co-ord	1/5/96	16	3
Stuart First	F	B	Whole-school policy	1/2/96	1/7/96	DHT/PT/HT	1/7/96	12	5
Stuart First	F	B/A	Circle time INSET	1/6/96	1/6/96	ALL	6/1/04	1.5	1
Wimple Chase	M	B	Class support Yr4	1/5/96	1/6/96	CT	6/1/04	2.5	3
Romsey First	F	B	Class support Yr2	1/4/96	1/5/96	CT	1/5/96	2	3
Elder High	S	B	Class support Yr10	1/2/96	1/5/96	CT	1/5/96	N/A	N/A
Buxford High	S	D	Boys Group Yr11	1/1/96	1/4/96	SENCO	1/4/96	N/A	N/A
Greenwoods	SS	D	Residential trip	1/5/96	1/6/96	CT	1/6/96	105	2
Hadrian School	SS	B	Midday supervisor INSET	1/5/96	1/6/96	MDS/SMT	1/10/96	12	10
Hilltop Middle/First	F/M	B	LSA INSET	1/5/96	1/5/96	LSAs	1/5/96	N/A	N/A
West Barnes High	S	B	NQT SUPPORT	1/4/96	1/7/96	NQTs	1/7/96	N/A	N/A

Key

School: school name

Phase: F = first, S = secondary, M = middle, SS = special school

Focus: B = behaviour, A = attendance, D = disaffection

Intervention: description of intervention, e.g. Class Yr4 team teaching, group work Yr11, Midday supervisor training

Start date: date at which intervention begins

Ant. end: date at which the project is intended to finish

Staff involved: School staff involved in delivering the project, i.e. CT = class teacher, HOY = Head of Year etc.

End date: Date when the project actually finished [it can be worth monitoring the overall slippage rates for closing project work and identifying reasons for time slip]

No. of hours: total number of hours from the behaviour support service used in delivering intervention. This should include direct contact and all preparation time

No. of visits: total number of direct visits for the delivery of the project

Figure 4.4 Example database – Project work

Initial	SSD	School	B/A	NCYr	M/F	SEN	Ethn.	DoR	Source	ABSS	DoC	Outcome	Exc	CoP	Hrs
CB	N	LINK TREE FIRST	B	R	M	3	3	23/4/99	SC	Paula	16/10/99	Maintained	X	3	48
DW	N	ST MARY'S	B	3	F	3	1	30/4/99	SC	Juliet	16/7/99	Maintained	X	2	26
LF	Y*	RUTLISH	B	8	M	2	1	5/5/99	EXH	Emma	3/2/00	Left area	X	3	76
MR	N	ALL SAINTS	B	10	M	3	1	14/6/99	SP	Gill	15/7/00	School leaver		3	114
TG	Y	CHILTERN FIRST	B	3	M	5	2	26/7/99	SO	Annette	16/9/99	Maintained		5	10
KMc	Y	HILLTOP MIDDLE	A	6	F	5	3	8/9/99	O	Mary	13/11/99	Special Sch.		5	12
JA	N	ST MATTHEW	B	N	M	5	3	10/10/99	SP	Bev	13/2/00	Maintained	X	3	21

Key

Initial: Pupil initial [NB This might be substituted for a referral number or unique identification number]

SSD: Is the pupil known to social services? Where an * is used this denotes that the child is in Public Care

School: School at which the pupil is on roll at the time of referral

B/A: Has the pupil been referred for concern primarily about behaviour (B) or attendance (A)?

NCYr: National Curriculum year group at point of referral [NB An additional field might be included for date of birth].

M/F: Pupil gender

SEN: Stage of the SEN Code of Practice at point of referral

Ethnicity: [LEAs vary in the codings that are used]

DoR: Date of referral

Source: The route through which the referral came: SC = school via an initial consultancy period; SP = school via project work; SO = school via another route; EXH = via the Exclusion Hotline (see previous chapter for explanation of this service); PPP = via the LEA Pupil Placement Panel; O = Other

ABSS: Allocated behaviour support worker

DoC: Date of closure

Outcome: Pupil destination and/or case resolution

Exc: Indicates whether the pupil was excluded during the period of support

CoP: SEN stage at the end of the support period

Hours: Total number of support hours for the case

Figure 4.5 Example database – Individual pupil work

Having established a system for collating key monitoring data it was important to ensure that the data fields corresponded with the partnership planning pro forma to minimise the administrative burden in data entry. Similarly, casework files for both project and individual pupil support were also designed for caseworkers to 'catch' data with minimal additional effort. Consequently a space for tallying up the total number of hours and visits was included to make totalling inputs straightforward (an example of a file record is provided in Figure 4.6).

Date of contact: **BSS team:**

Type of contact: Phone   Home   School   Other

Details:

Action: **Time:**

Date of contact: **BSS team:**

Type of contact: Phone   Home   School   Other

Details:

Action: **Time:**

Total hours this page: *Total visits this page:*

Total hours carried from previous: *Total visits carried from previous:*

New total: *New total:*

Figure 4.6 Sample file record

The result of this arrangement meant that gathering important operational data was well integrated into casework management:

- Team members were not able to deliver support unless it had been partnership planned (from which baseline profile, monitoring and evaluation data could be taken).
- Team members were expected to maintain case notes (which involved recording input data).
- Cases were not closed until the partnership plan had been reviewed (which secured the all important outcome data, including qualitative and quantitative data).

There were two advantages to operating this type of monitoring system. First, it was possible to generate regular reports on the number of projects and pupils being supported, with a breakdown of details about the nature of intervention and heavy/light user schools. It also provided useful information regarding team caseloads for management purposes. Second, the monitoring data formed a central element in the evaluation of the overall service.

Case study: Evaluation

In the same case study service evaluation was undertaken every year. Each exercise included a review of how effective the service had been in addressing its key objectives. Where possible, additional theme(s) would be considered (for example, in one year it was decided to carry out a specific enquiry into the development of non-unit based provision for disaffected pupils educated outside of school). The purpose of the evaluation exercise was threefold:

- to assess the extent to which the service had been meeting its key objectives;
- to provide key operational data to support local and national funding requirements, i.e. Single Regeneration Bid (SRB) reporting, Standards Fund monitoring;
- to identify areas for future service development.

The process for the evaluation exercise, which was actually implemented in the summer term, began in the latter half of the previous autumn term. A small working group drawn from the team set out the parameters of the evaluation including:

- clarification of evaluation focus;
- anticipated time-frame;
- methodology;
- allocation of tasks;
- involvement of external body to validate evaluation findings.

The activity of the group was time-limited and tightly focused. The purpose was to ensure that service evaluation took place, was well planned and had a high profile within the team. The evaluation action plan was presented to senior officers for endorsement before initiating the next steps which were more detailed planning of methodological tasks. An illustration of a possible process for service evaluation is presented in Figure 4.7.

Autumn term	Establish evaluation working group
	Clarify aims and objectives of evaluation exercise:
	• intended audience, e.g. Department for Education and Skills, LEA, schools • scope of the exercise, e.g. focus on project work, involvement of parents, specific interventions
	Identify third party involvement, e.g. independent consultant, inspectorate team
	Liaise with senior officers and school consultation groups to ensure compatibility with other pending consultation/evaluation activities
Spring term	Draft and finalise questionnaire formats, interview schedules
Summer term (first half)	Distribute questionnaires for return by half-term break
Summer term (second half)	Chase outstanding questionnaires
	Conduct interviews via third party
	Update service monitoring systems, e.g. partnership plans, GAS marks, individual files
	Collate questionnaires and interview responses
Autumn term	Publish and disseminate evaluation document

Figure 4.7 Sample evaluation process

The spring term was the period during which interview schedules, questionnaires and any school/pupil sampling were carried out. It was also necessary at this stage to plan the commissioning of a third party to either validate the evaluative material and/or carry out interviews for moderation purposes. In one year the evaluation involved drawing evidence from three central sources:

- all monitoring data for the full academic year collated from the service's internal filing system;
- survey material – questionnaire responses from all schools receiving support, an example of which is included at the end of this section;
- quantitative data from the LEA regarding attendance and exclusions per school.

In addition an external consultant was contracted to carry out a series of interviews with schools using a schedule similar to the questionnaire, which could then corroborate or contradict survey findings. In a previous year the service had invited the LEA inspectorate team to offer a critical perspective on methodology and moderate the validity of the final report. This had an additional benefit in increasing the awareness of the inspectorate team of the work of the behaviour support service.

Some of the learning points picked up over a series of evaluation exercises included:

- Keeping the focus of evaluation tightly focused. It was tempting to crowd interview schedules and questionnaires with all sorts of highly specific questions about a range of interventions but this would have greatly reduced the potential for drawing common findings in responses and would have had an impact on response rates. Consequently there were two clear dimensions to questions:
  - What impact has the service had on improving pupil, teacher and school behaviour?
  - How effective has the service approach been to referral, partnership planning and review?
- Presenting the school with a format that included both a space for comments and a rating system generated both qualitative and quantitative responses which was helpful.
- In addition to distributing the survey pro forma, each school was provided with a summary of the support it had received during the year. This proved useful for most schools where either intervention had been infrequent and possibly not recent, or where schools had received a high level of different types of support. In general it was a valuable tactic in demonstrating to schools the extent to which they had been supported over a whole year. This information was taken from the service monitoring system.
- Although more expensive, providing stamped addressed envelopes for returning school surveys was associated with a higher response rate.
- Particular care needed to be taken in canvassing the views of children and parents/carers. In most cases it was necessary for the support teacher to talk through the process and questionnaire.
- Where schools were asked to respond the questionnaire was addressed to the head teacher. However, to ensure an accurate response it was necessary to encourage a *school* response (as opposed to a head teacher response) by suggesting discussions with the main contact staff for the service, e.g. SENCO, HOY, took place prior to returning the questionnaire.

The questionnaires and interviews were carried out across the summer term and individual team members were committed to ensuring that case files were updated by the end of term. The remaining task was for all raw data to be sifted and drafted into the final evaluation report. The report was distributed to all schools and key agencies in addition to LEA officers and members.

The case study illustrates one possible approach to combining monitoring data with evaluation that has a clear focus on assessing a systemic model of behaviour support. Importantly, partnership planning lies at the heart of the strategy and is inextricably linked with identifying high quality outcomes.

5 Behaviour support: possibilities

In drawing this book to a close I want to briefly mention some final ideas for supporting systemic change, raise some notes of caution for intrepid behaviour support teams and finish with some hopeful thoughts. In preparing this summary chapter I have also attempted to draw together a series of observations from my work with a number of LEA services, outreach teams and on-site units from around the country. On the basis of this experience I have tried to make some sense of what kind of future might be in store for behaviour support.

Perhaps in many respects the art of the most effective behaviour support specialist is in being 'creatively subversive', to use a phrase from Gerda Hanko. It is a delicious phrase which acknowledges the sometimes twilight world of school behaviour and pupil disaffection but indicates a spirit of innovation and radicalism. Systemic strategies for responding to problem behaviour in schools are almost by definition creatively subversive in that solution-focused thinking can be highly challenging in an organisational culture preoccupied with blame and diagnosis. However, such an approach can also offer alternative perspectives to well-entrenched difficulties breathing new energy into tired and despairing teachers and children.

If behaviour support teams are to be really effective it may be best to regard their work as being akin to that of change agents. These colleagues are at one and the same time both part of an organisation, understanding its culture and dynamics, while also being outside of it and aware of limitations and potential for change. At its most effective the work of the behaviour support worker is a complex and subtle combination of diplomat, tactician and technical specialist with an additional high degree of self-awareness. It is perhaps worth drawing on other useful insights from Hanko to help us in understanding our role as agents of change. When under pressure 'systems resist what they need most' and 'creative subversion' can be a highly effective response. In developing such a strategy the advice is 'to always work with the healthy parts of the system'.

Another source of useful advice for behaviour support teams interested in developing systemic change is offered by Schmuck *et al.* (1977) and is presented in Figure 5.1 from material provided by Chris Watkins. I have made some additional comments in parentheses where appropriate.

These rules certainly reflect much of the spirit of the material covered in the previous chapters and give a clear picture of what type of approaches effective behaviour support specialists might use in carrying out their work. The rules

---

Rule 1: **Stay Alive**

Avoid self-sacrifice and nurture your aliveness.

(Whatever pressure team managers face, it is imperative to maintain the team meetings, the supervision sessions and professional development opportunities for behaviour specialists.)

Rule 2: **Start Where the System Is**

Establish empathy, build rapport and form understanding.

(The convention that uniformity equates with equity is outdated and the notion of a one-sized approach to behaviour support is no longer sustainable. The material on school culture and effective engagement in Chapter 2 is useful in meeting this need.)

Rule 3: **Never Work Uphill**

Don't build hills as you go, e.g. through building resistance to change.
Work in the most promising arena.
Build on resources, e.g. teams and partners.
Don't over-organise.
Don't argue if you can't win.

Rule 4: **Innovation Requires a Good Idea, Initiative and a Few Friends**

Find the people who are ready and able to work, introduce them to one another and work with them.

(An especially useful pointer when the behaviour support team is brokering multi-agency input to schools.)

Rule 5: **Load Experiments for Success**

Choose reliable partners: rebels may take the wrong risks and good soldiers don't take any.
Choose a variable level of risk and then take precautions to succeed.

Rule 6: **Light Many Fires**

With a wide range of partners – change programmes with one theme have high visibility and become good targets for resistance.

Rule 7: **Keep an Optimistic Bias**

Avoid being flooded by the destructive and conflictual aspects of problem situations.

Rule 8: **Capture the Moment**

(Schmuck *et al.* 1977)

Figure 5.1 Rules for change agents

of thumb are rooted in an optimistic and enthusiastic perspective which can be surprising for colleagues more familiar with despair and pessimism when responding to problem behaviour.

A sense of passion and belief is a prerequisite for pursuing a systems-based approach to behaviour support. It is important not least because of the factors that can most threaten the impact of the approach. Peggy Gosling is a behaviour support teacher in an inner London LEA team. For the past several years she has been investigating what makes for effective behaviour support as the focus for a doctoral thesis. As part of her work Peggy investigated a number of services with a view to understanding how it was that they were successful and what this might mean in terms of increasing effective practice. The conclusions of her work are in part quite chilling.

> ...my research has collected data from a dying breed. None of the 14 services...survives today. While I have no doubt that good practice goes on in pockets all over the country, there has been no framework within which this good practice has been recognised or allowed to flourish, locally or nationally. This represents a national contradiction to a further principle of the government's policy agenda, the commitment to evidence-based practice...services which were evidence-based and which have demonstrated effectiveness have gone. (Gosling 2001)

Gosling's reference to a dying breed connects with some of my introductory comments regarding the trend towards the cutting back of LEA-based teams and the drive towards greater delegation of budgets, particularly in the secondary sector. But there is perhaps another, more subtle reason for why it is that effective behaviour support may sometimes fail to survive. Gosling continues:

> It may be that effective behaviour support services had to go because we touched on debates and played out at school and LEA levels a clash of cultures in which the school improvement agenda has been powerfully held by inspectors and advisory services, staffed substantially by ex-head teachers. The perspective they brought to school improvement was concerned with simply good teaching and attainment targets and did not necessarily include the socially vulnerable children whom they themselves had excluded. Perhaps these services had to go because they threatened and challenged the beliefs of this very powerful group. Moreover they were caught in the crossfire between the inspectorate and LEA officers...The power of research and evidence stood for nothing in this game.
> (Gosling 2001)

So, for the intrepid behaviour support specialists here is a note of caution. We become more effective in our role as we increasingly raise issues of school improvement and performance. Quality behaviour support involves making closer links between the behaviour of children and that of adults and with the broader process of teaching and learning. Ultimately best practice in terms of behaviour support means asking questions of organisational culture, norms and values whether at school or LEA level. In pursuing this the behaviour specialists find themselves extending their partnership beyond the familiar network of educational psychologists and welfare officers, SENCOs, mentors and class assistants. Instead they begin knocking on the doors of powerful decision-makers: head teachers, governing bodies, school inspectors and LEA officers. The news we have may not be welcome. If we choose to take a systems approach to behaviour support we need to remain aware that there can be implications when exposing longstanding and well-established ways of understanding school behaviour and pupil disaffection. For colleagues working in LEA services, engaging collaboratively with the school improvement service must become a priority if behaviour support is to be both effective and sustainable. For colleagues working from specialist provision it is likewise important to locate outreach work in the thinking of leadership teams of both mainstream and special sector if work is to be seen as credible and worthwhile. For colleagues working in on-site provision it is imperative that Heads of Department and senior managers are involved from the outset in setting up in-school arrangements.

Finally, developing effective behaviour support can be about embracing and supporting the introduction of what are arguably some of the most alternative and innovative aspects of practice in education. The margins of the education system have always been the arena for experimental work and in the current context it seems as if there are opportunities to mainstream some of the best examples of different practice. Emotional literacy, nurture groups, in-school behaviour support services, dynamic on-site provision, mentorship, curriculum diversity in Key Stage 4, involvement of voluntary organisations and the development of schools as a platform for multi-agency service delivery are a few of the more exciting developments in education today. And behaviour support can be at the heart of this.

A recent example of what I mean by this is the work of the Gloucestershire secondary behaviour support team. As with several services around the country they have needed to consider how to work with schools that were setting up in-school centres. The tendency in some other areas has been for the local team to be invited to work with groups of children or individuals based at the unit. The Gloucester team, working on systems-based principles, deliberately focused their energies on supporting schools in the negotiation and contracting process of setting up provision. The message to behaviour support teams is clear enough – do not wait around for an initiative to be up and running before becoming involved; be part of setting up the system in the first place.

> The zeitgeist has never been more responsive to taking on and seeing through [the challenges of disaffection]. Today teetering on the brink of the new millennium, there is a constellation of possibilities out there waiting to be explored, tried and tested. Maybe it has taken getting to the stage where our backs are against the wall, where the sheer volume of the problems has forced us to look them in the face...
>
> However you choose to look at it, the time has come to embrace new thinking, methodologies and practices to bring marginalised and troubled young people out from the shadows and into school communities that are better geared to accommodate, care for and inspire them. Teaching young people who don't want to be taught can be the most thankless, frustrating

task in the world. But when you transform the system...so that school is a compelling place where children and young people can experience success and progress, where they can make connections that help them understand, where they feel they have a valuable contribution to make and where they are valued for who they are, there's nothing quite like it.　(Klein 1999)

There has never been a better time to develop behaviour support. Service delivery may not take the format that it has in the past but the sense of vocation that has driven many people into the field of behaviour support remains as important now as over the past 20 years. Perhaps, however, there might be a renewed emphasis in the focus for support as well as a wider range of vehicles through which it is delivered. Maybe, as teachers, schools, LEAs and government departments struggle to reconcile the apparent contrary standards and inclusion agendas, the valuable contribution of systemic behaviour support will be recognised.

I will finish as I started, with a story from my own experience. I had the good fortune to manage a splendid team of behaviour support professionals, all of whom were committed to the principles of systemic approaches. A frequent area of discussion for the team – and sometimes the root of an anxiety – was whether in the quest to develop school systems and staff confidence, we lost sight of the vulnerable child. Occasionally though there were cases that illustrated quite succinctly just how powerful systemic theory might be in its impact on the emotional experience of children and teachers.

One of the behaviour support teachers on the team became involved in a piece of work that was ostensibly about an individual pupil in a local first school. Apparently the child – about six years old – was highly disruptive and everyone was running out of hope for the case. The support teacher engaged with the class teacher and over a period of time introduced a familiar behavioural system, based on specific rule reinforcement with incremental rewards. Perhaps what made the work distinctive was that the support teacher never worked with the child, but focused instead on the concerns raised by the class teacher. The intervention was essentially about addressing the perceptions of staff and realising their hopes through working with their resourcefulness.

The ultimate goal for the child was to take part in the school Christmas play. And so it came to pass that he achieved his target and played his part. As was customary at the school, all the children taking part lined up for a post-production photograph. The moment the shutter clicked the boy burst with joy, sprang up from his place, held his arms up high and called out to all that might hear him an almighty 'Yes!'

He had never known the support teacher, and the credit was his and his class teacher's to share. But it was a textbook case of quality effective behaviour support, nevertheless.

References

Barrow, G. (1998) *Dealing with Disaffection: Merton's mainstream approach to difficult behaviour.* Bristol: Centre for Studies on Inclusive Education.

Barrow, G., Howard, P. and Hrekow, P. (2001a) *Learning Support Units: A practical guide to setting up and developing in-school provision.* London: Dreyfus Training & Development Ltd. Available from PO Box 886, Morden, Surrey SM4 4AL.

Barrow, G., Bradshaw, E. and Newton, T. (2001b) *Improving Behaviour and Raising Self-Esteem in the Classroom: A Practical Guide to Using Transactional Analysis.* London: David Fulton Publishers.

Bennathan, M. and Boxall, M. (1998) *The Boxall Profile: A guide to effective intervention in the education of pupils with emotional and behavioural difficulties.* Maidstone: Association of Workers for Children with Emotional and Behavioural Difficulties.

Bertalanffy, L. von (1968) *General Systems Theory: Foundation, Development, Applications.* New York: Braziller.

Birmingham LEA (1998) *Behaviour in Schools: Framework for Intervention.* Birmingham: Birmingham City Council.

Critchley, B. and Casey, D. (1989) 'Organisations get stuck too', *Leadership and Organisational Development Journal* **10**, 4.

DES (1989) *Discipline in Schools.* Report of the Elton enquiry. London: Department of Education and Science.

DfEE (1999) *Social Inclusion: Pupil Support.* London: Department for Education and Employment.

English, F. (1975) 'The three-cornered contract', *Transactional Analysis Journal* **5**.

Faupel, A. W. (1990) 'A Model Response to Emotional and Behavioural Development in Schools', *Educational Psychology in Practice* **5**, 4.

Gilligan, R. (1998) 'The importance of schools and teachers in child welfare', *Child and Family Social Work* **3**.

Gosling, P. (2001) *Partnership for Change: Effective behaviour support* (Unpublished doctoral dissertation).

Gray, P., Noakes, J. and Miller, A. (1994) *Challenging Behaviour in Schools: Teacher support, practical techniques and policy developments.* London: Routledge.

Hallam, S. and Castle, F. (1999) *Evaluation of the behaviour and discipline pilot projects (1996–9) supported under the standards fund programme.* DfEE Research Brief (RR163).

Hamill, P. and Boyd, B. (2001) 'Rhetoric or Reality? Inter-agency provision for young people with challenging behaviour', *Emotional and Behavioural Difficulties* **6**, 3.

Hanko, G. (1999) *Increasing Competence through Collaborative Problem Solving.* London: David Fulton Publishers.

Hay, J. (1995) *Donkey Bridges for Developmental TA: Making transactional analysis memorable and accessible*. Watford: Sherwood Publishing.

Haynes, J. (1999) *Starting to Join: A baseline study of multi-agency activity*. Berkshire: NFER.

Huskins, J. (1999) *From Disaffection to Social Inclusion: A social skills approach to developing active citizenship and lifelong learning*. London: UK Youth 2nd Floor, Kirby House, 20–24 Kirby Street, London EC1N 8TS.

Jolly M. and McNamara, E. (1991) *Towards Better Behaviour: Part 1. The Behaviour Survey Checklist*. Available from TBB, 10 Sandygate Lane, Broughton, Preston, Lancs. PR3 5LA.

Jolly M. and McNamara, E. (1992) *Towards Better Behaviour: Part 2. Assessment*. Available from TBB, 7 Quinton Close, Ainsdale, Merseyside PR8 2TD.

Kinder, K., Wilkin, A., Moor, H., Derrington, C. and Hogarth, S. (1999) *Raising Behaviour 3. A School View*. Berkshire: NFER.

Klein, R. (1999) *Defying Disaffection: How schools are winning the hearts and minds of reluctant students*. Staffordshire: Trentham Books.

Lacey, P. and Lomas, J. (1993*) Support Services and the Curriculum: A Practical Guide to Collaboration*. London: David Fulton Publishers.

Leggett, N. (2000) 'Supporting Secondary Schools to Manage Emotional and Behavioural Difficulties', *Emotional and Behavioural Difficulties* **5**, 2.

Long, R. and Fogell, J. (1999) *Supporting Pupils with Emotional Difficulties: Creating a Caring Environment for All*. London: David Fulton Publishers.

McGuire, J. and Richman, N. (1988) *Pre-School Behaviour Checklist*. Windsor: NFER-Nelson.

McSherry, J. (2001) *Challenging Behaviours in Mainstream Schools: Practical strategies for effective intervention and reintegration*. London: David Fulton Publishers.

Micholt, N. (1992) 'Psychological Distance and Group Interventions', *Transactional Analysis Journal* **24**, 4.

Molnar, A. and Lindquist, B. (1989) *Changing Problem Behaviour in Schools*. San Francisco: Jossey-Bass Publishers.

O'Hanlon, B. and Beadle, S. (2000) *A Field Guide to Possibility Land: Possibility Therapy Methods*. London: BT Press.

Porter, L. (2000) *Behaviour in Schools: Theory and Practice for Teachers*. Philadelphia: Open University Press.

Provis, M. (1992) *Dealing with Difficulty: A systems approach to problem behaviour*. London: Hodder & Stoughton.

Rennie, E. (1993) 'Evaluating Behaviour Support: A Consideration of Possibilities', *Educational Psychology in Practice* **9**, 1, April.

Schmuck, R. A. *et al.* (1977*) Second Handbook of Organisation Development in Schools*. Mountain View: Mayfield Publishing Company.

Stringer, B. and Mall, M. (1999) *A Solution Focussed Approach to Anger Management With Children, A Group Work Manual for Practitioners*. Birmingham: The Questions Publishing Company Ltd.

Tyler, K. (1998) Changing Chronic Behaviour in Primary Schools, *The Person Centred Journal* **5**, 2.

Ware, P. (1983) 'Personality Adaptions – Doors to Therapy', *Transactional Analysis Journal* **13**, 1, January.

Watkins, C. and Wagner, P. (2000) *Improving School Behaviour*. London: Paul Chapman Publishing.

Index